SOCIETY'S VICTIM—THE POLICEMAN

*to achieve peace of mind and fulfillment through
self-expression, most men need a commitment to work
in the service of some cause that they can respect*
—**Hans Selye**

to the over 450,000 members of the workforce
comprising that occupation known as policing

SOCIETY'S VICTIM—THE POLICEMAN

AN ANALYSIS OF
JOB STRESS IN POLICING

By

WILLIAM H. KROES, Ph.D.

Director, Institute for Stress Management
Los Angeles, California
Formerly,
Chief, Stress Research Section
National Institute for Occupational
Safety and Health
Cincinnati, Ohio

CHARLES C THOMAS • PUBLISHER

Springfield • Illinois • U.S.A.

Published and Distributed Throughout the World by
CHARLES C THOMAS • PUBLISHER
Bannerstone House
301-327 East Lawrence Avenue, Springfield, Illinois, U.S.A.

© 1976, by CHARLES C THOMAS • PUBLISHER

ISBN 0-398-03479-6

Library of Congress Catalog Card Number: 75 22118

Library of Congress Cataloging in Publication Data
Kroes, William H
  Society's victim, the policeman.
  Bibliography: p.
  Includes index.
  1. Police—Diseases and hygiene. 2. Stress
(Psychology) —Case studies. I. Title.
HV7936.H4K76   1976   363.2'2   75-22118
ISBN 0-398-03479-6

This book was written by Dr. William Kroes in
his private capacity. No official support or endorse-
ment by the National Institute for Occupational
Safety and Health is intended or should be in-
ferred.

W-2
Printed in the United States of America

PREFACE

STOP ANY worker on the street and ask him his opinion on job stress, and the odds are he will reply something to the effect, "You want to talk about *stress*, let me tell you about *my* job . . . have I got stress," and so on into an animated pitch on the pressures of his job. As a researcher and clinician I have found over and over again that members of the work force (be they presidents of companies or janitors) are eager to discuss job stress. The reason for this is obvious. Job stress is a part of every worker's life.

During the last four years, I have viewed the job stresses in occupations ranging from roofing construction to underground coal mining. So, why write a book just on the occupation of policing? The answer is really fourfold. First, available morbidity and mortality data indicate that the police have more stress-related health problems than most other workers. Second, the police are subjected to certain job stressors which are unique and because of their uniqueness help shed light on the whole area of psychological stress and its consequences. Third, the police profession is an occupation in which many stresses can be alleviated, once the public becomes aware of their insidious nature and the role the public itself plays in creating them. Last, I have been encouraged by police professionals and consultants to put my views on paper to help overcome the lack of awareness of the public and, to my surprise, many police administrators who do not realize how much job stress can affect job performance and the lives of police personnel and their families. Hopefully, this book will ultimately lead to a reduction of some of the terrible stressors policemen must face daily.

INTRODUCTION

—for the Police Officer

It is always a difficult task for an outsider to offer, to the experienced worker, information concerning his own job, and in this case it is especially tough. Few other professions have had as many behavioral scientists and psychiatrists wandering through administering questionnaires along the way, lecturing on "how it ought to be done," organizing sensitivity workshops, restructuring the job, riding around observing police-citizen interactions, holding retreats, offering "expert" consulting services, and gathering material for professional articles. And afterward you are at best left in the same position as when you started, perhaps a bit more tired and frustrated. It is little wonder that you become skeptical. Consequently, the least I can do at the start is to tell you what I am about and what benefits you may derive from reading this book. I am a specialist in the area of the effects of job stress on the worker, especially on his health. The term health is used here in its broadest sense implying not only the absence of disease, but dis-EASE itself, including one's well-being and positive mental health. I have looked at a variety of professions, and found stress elements in them all. Several years ago I began to study policing, ostensibly because of the many reports that I had received on the severe health disorders associated with the occupation, but really for reasons that probably lie much deeper. My college days were spent at Berkeley in the early 1960s, and I "knew" what a policeman was—a pig. Only as I attained professional maturity did I stop to reexamine my attitude. As I began to realize how deeply the negative public attitudes affect policemen, I began to concentrate my research effort on this occupation.

Tragically, I found that many of the stressors in policing need not be; they are *not inherent in the nature of police work* and can be alleviated. As a consequence, this book is written in an attempt to bring the serious problems of police job stress into your and the public's awareness and to point out what ameliorative steps can be taken.

It is hoped that this book will serve as a supplement to your cadet or in-service training, or if need be, as a substitute for the training you should have received but did not, to prepare you to cope with the negative influences of the job on your well-being. It is my strong wish that the information presented here will be useful in either reducing the stress load you bear or in helping you to adapt better to it.

I should hope that those of you who have risen to the rank of lieutenant, captain, or even chief will feel a special responsibility. Many of the stressors an individual policeman faces can best be dealt with organizationally. It is hoped that you will use this book as a management guide to reduce the unnecessary stresses on your subordinates. By so doing, you will receive dividends in the form of increased efficiency in your organization and decreased crime rates in areas under your jurisdiction.

—for the General Public

Where do we get our attitudes about policing and the policeman? Chances are they come from several sources: the many television shows, there are over two dozen new ones planned for the fall, 1975 season; movies that portray the cop as a super hero or super villain; the frequently biased newspaper headlines and editorials; the newsreels showing confrontations between police and students or racial minorities; or even from our own reactions to the one traffic ticket we received from a police officer. But the fact is that almost without exception, no outsider knows what it is really like to be a police officer. We view policemen as we view an iceberg; we fail to see the most important three-quarters.

What you are about to read may come as a surprise to you and may even be unsettling, but I hope it will help you to develop a truer picture of the policeman and his work. At a minimum

you should gain an understanding of what burdens the officer
must shoulder, how powerful the job stressors in policing are,
and how profoundly they affect police officers and their families.

Figure 1. The Real Policeman

ACKNOWLEDGMENTS

To Joseph J. Hurrell, Jr., the student who knew more than the teacher, for his invaluable help, and to John R. P. French, Jr. and Robert Caplan whose pioneering work in the field of job stress research has helped me over innumerable hurdles. Also, a special vote of gratitude to the many policemen and police consultants who have given freely of their valuable time so that I may learn. Finally, I would like to thank Hans Selye, through whose works and advice I have gained further insights into the world of stress.

CONTENTS

SOCIETY'S VICTIM—THE POLICEMAN

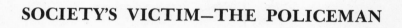

CHAPTER 1 JOB STRESS

WORK, FOR MOST OF US, is an important part of our lives, and it is only too true that our jobs play a central role in our overall health and happiness. There is a growing awareness in America today of this profound impact of work on the lives and welfare of people and the high cost of dissatisfied workers to industry and society. Together with this growing awareness is the emergence of a philosophy which emphasizes the right of all workers to meaningful and healthy jobs. The effects of employee discontent are becoming well-known. Extensive research studies show, for example, that the most important factor in ensuring longevity is not overall life satisfaction, medical history, or even a doctor's examination, but job satisfaction. For the author, the most dramatic evidence of the centrality of work in our lives comes from the research of a Swedish cardiologist, Torres Theorell, who found that in discussing various topics with patients who had survived a myocardial infarct (heart attack) and in monitoring their brain wave, electrocardiogram (ECG), only the topic of work produced arrythmias high enough to produce another heart attack. The topics of family, sex life, disease problems, and even financial condition produced little change in the ECG. Only the topic of work consistently produced dangerous arrythmias.

Albert Camus once said, "Without work all life goes rotten. But when work is soulless, life stifles and dies." This quote stands as the introduction to the final report of a committee, composed of sixty-eight of the most widely recognized authorities on work. The overall recommendation of this committee's report (*Work in America,* 1973) was that a major priority of industry today should be to make jobs more satisfying for the American workers.

What is it about jobs that make them less than satisfying? Simply put, it is the negative pressures and stressors of the job that lead to worker dissatisfaction. And though the committee on Work in America did not single out the profession of policing to acknowledge the problems therein, if they had looked into this profession they would have found that policing is one of the

3

most difficult jobs in America today, and the workers in this profession are experiencing unbelievably high amounts of negative work pressures and job stress.

To understand this most significant problem in policing one needs to know more about what job stress is. It may be defined as the occupational pressures or burdens which adversely affect workers. This definition is not as elegant as the more sophisticated psychosocial ones, or those which posit a medical-biochemical model, but it serves to reinforce an important point—that, what is troublesome, overwhelming, or uncomfortable about a job can be labelled the stress of that job. The aggregate of individual troublesome factors linked with any particular job is the total job stress associated with that job. For convenience the specific individual negative factors are called job *stressors.*

Job stress is not a rare entity. Like the common cold, we all experience its discomfort. The garbage collector tells you that he has a stressful job, and upon examination one can easily identify several significant psychological job stressors, such as low job status, underutilization of skills, repetitive and boring work, and so on. The air line pilot will say that, "Man, do I have job stress" and proceed to enumerate stressors which are significant to his job: responsibility for the lives and welfare of people, "jet lag," and so on. The air traffic controller thinks the garbage collector and air line pilot have "cushy" jobs because his job stressors, such as changing shift routines, information overload, and extreme responsibility for the lives of others, are even more overpowering. And so it goes, almost becoming a game of who has the most ulcers. But that is just the point. The stress associated with any particular job or profession can have a powerful negative effect on the individual in that job. But, it is a moot point whether one's definition of job stress is scientifically rigorous or not. It is more important to know that job stress exists and that it is a significant problem for workers in many occupations. And in the police profession, job stress not only exists, but it may be the *paramount* problem facing policemen today.

To show that a problem such as job stress exists is one thing, but in a practical sense, it is more important to do something about the problem. The first step in that direction should be to identify the individual job stressors within an occupation and determine their potential for harm to the individual worker. Once the individual job stressors have been identified, we may begin to develop meaningful ways to combat their negative effects.

This will be the approach taken in this book. Beginning with Chapter 2 we shall look at the individual job stressors in policing. Following this we will look at the combined effects of these stressors on the police officer and his family (Chap. 5) and conclude by looking at what can be done to reduce the effects of these stressors (Chap. 6). Before so doing, however, it is helpful to look at some of the theoretical issues and problems that invariably come up in a discussion of job stress.

The job stress referred to in this book is *psychological* job stress. In some work environments there may be physical, chemical, or other noxious hazards which can also be conceived of as stressors. For example, factory workers subjected to high noise levels may lose their hearing, or underground coal miners exposed to coal dust in the air may develop pneumoconious, commonly called black lung. But for many jobs the chemical and physical hazards are not of prime importance and may not even exist. In air traffic controlling, for example, one cannot find any chemical or physical hazards. Nevertheless, research and clinical-medical evidence shows that air traffic controllers suffer from higher rates of several health disorders (including ulcers) than most other workers. The stressors air traffic controllers experience are purely *psychological.*

Unlike the air traffic controller, the policeman faces certain physical hazards associated with his job, but, as will be shown in a later chapter, these nonpsychological stressors play only a small part in the health and well-being of the policeman. As Joseph Wambaugh, the crusading cop-author, puts it, "Police work is not particularly dangerous physically; but the most dangerous job in the world emotionally."

At a recent international conference comprised of some of the world's leading stress researchers the proceedings became bogged down at one point over the issue of how much job stress is too much. It was concluded that without this "much needed information" it would be impossible to do anything about job stress. This point of view puzzles the author. For one thing, the job stressors in many jobs are so damaging that the question of what is the appropriate level is relatively unimportant; get the stress load down first. The more important issue is that for many stressors there is no optimum level; any amount of the stressor is bad. It is like air pollution; no amount is desirable, even though under a certain level we may still survive. Thus, whenever it is possible, job stress should be reduced. We should be alert to all the poisons and toxins in our environment, and job stress should be included in the list of environmental toxins. *Job stress, if you will, is a work hazard, too.* Our emphasis should be on reducing this stress hazard, not quibbling over the maximum acceptable level.

A variation on the above argument derives from the biological view that there is an optimum level of stress, and that too little as well as too much stress is bad. In terms of maintaining one's biological equilibrium or homeostasis, the author has no argument but to go the extra step and assume that job stress is essential to maintaining an optimum level of arousal is going too far. There are enough stimuli in our modern world to keep us aroused and going without adding toxic job stressors.

Another popular notion is that stress is good for you. Put another way, without stress one could not enjoy his job. As the poets and philosophers tell us, one who has not experienced pain cannot experience pleasure. Following is an example which may bring this argument into focus. Recently a rather well-known courtroom psychiatrist, who is also a concert violinist, stated that it was the stress in each of his jobs that provided the zest that made his life interesting. This same individual related that as a young doctor he voluntarily rode the emergency ambulance during his free time for the excitement, and as he put it, "If you don't think that is stressfull work . . ." Concerning the stress in his major occupations, he related that as a courtroom psychiatrist he must face the opposing attorney in a battle of wits and must always be alert. As a violin virtuoso he must face an audience, perform a multitude of fine hand movements without making a mistake, all the time holding a complicated and lengthy musical score in his memory. In short, from this individual's viewpoint, his job stress prevents his life from becoming dull and meaningless. Is he right? Is the author wrong? The problem here arises from the misuse of the word stress. What our violin playing psychiatrist is calling stress, a more scientific researcher would call *challenge*, which is an intrinsic job motivator. Facing an opponent in the courtroom for him is challenging and exciting. This is not a job stressor and can only be conceived as such for the individual who is petrified in a courtroom and who strongly dislikes doing battle with another. Similarly, performing on the concert stage is not only challenging to the psychiatrist, but it allows him to utilize a multitude of his abilities and satisfies his needs for achievement, activity, creativity, importance, personal growth and development, and recognition. These are job motivators, not job stressors. This is true also for riding the ambulance, an activity which can be exciting, rewarding, and challenging. Thus, one must be careful to distinguish between job stressors which negatively affect the worker and other factors which fulfill basic psychological needs, and provide the motivation and incentive to work.*

Lastly, there is the view held by all too many, that stress is good for a person as it helps to build character. This view often derives from the philosophy which holds the common man to be basically lazy and no-good. This approach holds that to be made more productive, moral, etc. the worker must be controlled and driven. This view was especially prevalent during the nineteenth century when unfair labor practices, such as child labor abuse, long working hours, and unsafe working conditions, were also prevalent. Today, it is not unusual to hear proponents of this view explain that they made it the hard way. The author wishes these "fortunate" individuals could see the thousands of humans broken from the effects of too much job stress.

The word fortunate is placed in quotation marks for a reason; how fortunate actually are those who have made it up the ladder of success through intense job stress? Take a look at the con-

---

*Hans Selye, a leading stress researcher, gets around this argument by considering stressors as being both positive and negative. When the stressor is positive, e.g. meeting a loved one after many years absence, or the stress a great conductor shows in his face when leading an orchestra, it is good, and stress when it is negative is bad. The former he calls stress, the latter he calls distress.

stricted personalities, rigid attitudes, and overall unhappiness of those who have made it the hard way. One well-known industrial psychologist who consults primarily with the executive elite recently remarked that he knows of no other group as depressed and unhappy as the successful executive, and he has dealt with hundreds of them.

We can, of course, grow from stressful, uncomfortable experiences, but it is more difficult. Why must we develop such serious artificial handicaps to our growth and fulfillment? Why must we create job stressors purposely? The research literature is replete with evidence showing that creativity and intelligence develop best in rewarding, enriching environments, and not in repressive, overpowering ones. So, who can honestly say that job stress is good for us? The author would like some of those individuals to step forward and share some of his more objectionable job stressors such as oppressive administrative overload, paperwork, and red tape, and then tell how rewarding it is and how it shapes character. It only makes him irritable. But if they were to offer their services, giving the author additional time to do what he considers to be more meaningful and rewarding tasks, how much happier he would be in his job.

But we must return now to the main theme of this chapter. It has been stated that job stress has certain negative consequences. The following will illustrate some of these. Figure 2 shows a solid citizen (the square block) holding down an ideal job. In this ideal job environment, no job stressors impinge upon him and so no negative effects or job *strains* result. Figures 3 and 4 depict the same worker who is now subject to job stressors which produce a strain to him. In essence, the stress of the job interacts with the worker to disrupt his psychological and physiological homeostasis, resulting in a strain effect. The strain effect may be varied, strong or weak, shortlived or long lasting, but there will *always be a strain effect*. The nature, extent, and duration of the strain effects as they lead to reduced efficiency at work, personality change, and medical conditions such as ulcers, heart attack, asthma, and obesity will be discussed in depth later in this book. In Figure 5 a simplified model depicting this view is presented.

IDEAL JOB ENVIRONMENT

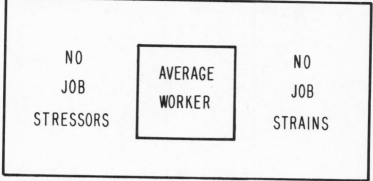

Figure 2. Average worker in ideal job environment.

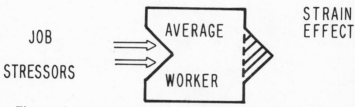

Figure 3. Average worker under conditions of job stress.

Figure 4. Effect of powerful or prolonged job stressors.

Figure 5. Relationship between job stress and strain: simplified model.

CHAPTER 2 STRESSORS SHARED WITH OTHER OCCUPATIONS

T O UNDERSTAND THE EFFECT of job stress on policemen it is helpful to divide the stressors a policeman faces into two categories: (1) stressors that policing has in common with other occupations and (2) unique stressors specific to the police profession. In this chapter the first class of stressors will be discussed.

Administration

The problem of administrative pressure on the individual worker is so ubiquitous across occupations that the author wonders if there is not some universal law of human nature operating to ensure that, for any organization employing thirty or more people, unnecessary rules, red tape, and a breakdown in communication between management and the workers will exist. Almost universally in large organizations there is a very real communication gap between those at the top and those at the bottom. This gap may be due to the usual inefficiencies of bureaucracy in large organization, or it may be due to the differences in conditions, influences, and factors that an individual must consider at different levels in the organization, e.g. the manager makes decisions and issues rules based on different information and from a different perspective than that of the worker. In any case, the stressor of administration is a very real problem for the policeman. Excessive paper work and red tape, lack of voice in decisions that vitally concern him (and which he may be uniquely qualified to make), antiquidated promotional policies, as well as other impediments and petty requirements interfere with and handicap the policeman in doing his job. Further, they serve as irritants that can grow into a major stressor.

Though the problem of administration is faced by many front-line workers in nearly all organizations, it is exceptionally significant for the policeman. Generally, this is so because of the organizational structure and evolved culture of the typical police department. Most police departments are organized on a quasi-paramilitaristic basis. As such the policeman faces the pressures of the average G.I.: excessive dress-code and hair-length regulations, problems of being low man on the totem pole, being required to show respect and respond properly to a superior officer, and so on. As Martin Reiser (1974), department psychologist for the Los Angeles Police Department, puts it:

> In the traditional police organization, authoritarian management approaches predominate with relatively little attention or concern being given to individual problems or human factors. Typically, the jackass fallacy is operative. This is based on the carrot and stick approach to personnel management, which assumes that without either dangling a tasty reward in front of someone's nose or beating him with a stick he will not move.

Administrative stress can be subdivided into two subcategories: (1) administrative policy concerning work assignments, procedures, and personal conduct and (2) lack of administrative backing and support of patrolmen, including the relationship and rapport between patrolmen and their administrators. Evidence, to date, indicates that negative feelings about administration policy far outweighs feelings of lack of administration support. Thus, the problem of administrator as bureaucrat appears to be a more bothersome problem to the average police officer than administrator as poor supervisor.* By administrators the author is referring to senior-level command personnel, i.e. lieutenants, captains, colonels, or the chief.

There are three problems that deserve special notice with regard to this stressor. Two, red tape and lack of say, fall within the administrative policy subcategory, and one, backing of policemen, falls within the administrative support subcategory.

Red Tape

Along with bureaucracy comes paper work, or as the man filling it out terms it, red tape. The amount of paperwork the policeman faces is remarkable. It is such a problem in policing, that

---

*As one officer stated upon retirement, He was sicker of fighting the "guys upstairs" than the hoodlums.

Watson and Sterling in a 1969 International Association of Chiefs of police survey of over 4,500 police officers found that they consider "too much paper work" as their major job-related problem.

Another finding of the survey was that over 67 percent of the officers agreed with the statement, "The best officer is one who knows when to depart from standard operating procedure in order to get the job done." A most sad commentary on the status of police administration.

Lack of Say

This problem, lack of a voice in decisions that vitally affect one's job and life, is a serious one for police officers. Examples of such situations are patrolmen being transferred from one partner to another or one duty assignment or district to another without any advance notice, or being told to follow prescribed procedure, or to use specific equipment by an administration quite distant from the actual situation. Anyone who had military experience appreciates the service expression for this problem: there is the right way, the wrong way, and the military way.

Lack of say also includes the frustration an officer feels when his skills are being either misused or not used at all. The highly trained crime fighter is often expected, for example, to direct traffic, give tickets, or even more appalling, undertake nonpolice activities such as investigating complaints about too many weeds growing in a property owner's lawn. Yet, there is a practical reason why police officers are required to undertake these activities. Cities are chronically strapped for funds and the various departments within the city must compete for the limited tax revenues. As a result of this in-fighting, agreements are reached between the department heads providing, for example, that the police will undertake a service for the health department, such as following up a dog bite complaint, which is a health department responsibility, for some other favor in return. Though there may be a logical reason for these nonpolice activities, it still does not make the professional policeman feel any better even if he is told the reasons. In fact, due to the bureaucracy communication barrier he often is not told. Again, before condemning police for their feelings, it is wise to consider how you would feel as a professional if you had to empty all wastebaskets and wash the windows or clean the restrooms.

The average policeman has received special training, has served an extended apprenticeship as a "rookie," and, therefore, understandably takes pride in his work. He perceives himself as, the trained law enforcement specialist that he is. Within this framework he develops a certain perception of himself, that of a *professional.**

Psychologically, it is very threatening and uncomfortable when a discrepancy occurs between one's self-perception and the perception of oneself by others. The officer sees himself as a knowledgeable expert providing a vital service to the community, but he is often treated as if he is an enemy to the well-being of the community. Thus, administrative support is needed to provide the officer with positive feedback.

An officer is better able to cope with the stress he faces if he feels that his superiors know and understand his problems and are in his corner. It is clear that to some extent line police feel let down by their administration. Instead of the administration's taking some pressures off the officers, they produce more by not letting the officer provide any professional input in decisions and policies that directly affect him. Thus, in several ways the individual officer perceives his own administration as failing to treat him as a professional.

Another important aspect of this stress centers around differences of opinion between an individual worker and his superiors. Only the individual in business for himself or the private consultant can escape this trying aspect. Because of the militaristic atmosphere within the police department, line police officers are discouraged from expressing opinions to their superiors. This is

---

*Some researchers prefer to restrict the use of the term professional to those engaged in the *learned* professions. However, the term is used here in the general sense of one following an occupation for which he receives special training and has special skills and competence not available to other groups of workers. Perhaps, a better definition is that given by George Bernard Shaw, "A professional is one who does his job well even if he doesn't feel like it."

especially difficult for the police officer, because, as mentioned before, the police officer has extensive professional training and feels he has important inputs to make. Further, the individual officer, even though he may be low man on the totem pole, is required to act quite independently when he is out on the streets. The supervisor is some miles away at headquarters and decisive action needs to be taken immediately. This independence of carrying out job function coupled with skilled training makes any suppression of one's opinions and inputs into the decision-making process difficult. But, the officer is seldom allowed to voice his opinion and must stomach it (where it rests and occasionally grows into an ulcer). Repeating this point again, because it does need emphasis, the police officer is highly trained and often has many years street experience as a professional, but his supervisor often treats him more in a father-son manner. The system discourages him from speaking, and so this conflict rests inside of him, sometimes in a state of silent rage.

Backing of Policemen

This problem relates mainly to *use of force* incidents. Occasions arise when an officer is called upon to use force, e.g. in quieting a bar room disturbance or apprehending a suspect. However, there is a fine line between judicious use of force and excessive use of force. Because of the public nature of these incidents, and the strong reaction of some segments of the public, extreme pressures are put on city hall and the police administration to investigate these incidents. An outsider to the police department cannot imagine the anguish the officer must go through during these interrogations. Knowing this potential problem, the officer needs also to know where his superiors stand; will they support and back him, or will they abandon him to the wolves? Many line officers will tell you that in the interest of public relations they are abandoned by their superiors. Note the following officer's comments:

> The officer is given a gun to protect himself and others, and indirectly from that point on the same authority that gave it to him tells him he is not responsible enough to use it. They give him pages of proce-

dures on when, where, how, and why to not use it. When he does, on remote occasion, have to resort to the weapon, he must submit himself to pages of paperwork, interrogations, and debates of public news media. This is a definite reflection on the officer's verasity, character and integrity and is a direct affront to his profession, as well as to himself.

When an incident such as this occurs to one patrolman, the feeling of helplessness and lack of support spreads to the others. As a result, a general feeling of mistrust of the administration develops among the rank and file. There is an established belief among police officers that when there is praise to be given a department, some superior steps out of the woodwork to receive it, but when there is punishment it falls downhill to the lowest level, the field police officer.

This added anxiety of not knowing where one stands complicates the officer's reaction to a situation in which his help is needed. Not infrequently, a policeman must make a split-second decision on the street. Knowing that there might be a future hearing to decide whether his actions were proper or not, places the officer in a most difficult situation. In order to avoid future disapproval from superiors, officers sometimes avoid action and let the problem continue. By not stepping in, the officers allow lawlessness to grow. But can we blame the policeman for "not doing his duty"? Look at our own situations; if we do not know where we stand with our administrators, we often fail to act. We, too, have careers to think about, and we too do not want to get on the bad side of our superiors. Thus, we are all guilty, at times, of being less effective than we could be on our jobs. Taking the easy way out arises not from laziness, but a reaction, well-documented by behavioral research, which shows that our actions are shaped by the rewards and punishments provided by our environment. And in the work environment the rewards and punishments are carefully controlled.

One may question why use of force is included in this chapter on stressors shared with other occupations. Few of us are authorized to use guns, clubs, or mace, so, why is such authority not considered a police specific stressor? The answer is that though the specifics of the incidents may vary from occupation to occupation, the problem of administration support is the same.

A coal miner, for example, may not report a safety violation because it will anger his foreman, or a subordinate will not report to his boss that things are going bad for fear of being unfairly blamed as the harbinger of bad tidings, or the factory foreman will not take some needed action because it may be considered controversial and he is not sure of his superior's support, and the policeman will not use force fearing his superiors will not back him.

It should be noted that others feel the administration stressor to be so important that they separate it into several distinct stress categories. For example, Terry Eisenberg, based on his own experience as a police officer, identified 30 sources of psychological stress, five of which (poor supervision, lack of career development, inadequate reward/reinforcement system, offensive administrative policy, and excessive paper work) I group under the administration stressor.

Job Conflict

Job conflict refers to the situation in which an individual is caught between discordant expectations. These discordant expectations may be either a conflict in demands placed on him by others or a conflict between his own needs and those of others. This stressor can take many forms and arises under a variety of situations, such as the conflict arising from having in effect, two bosses. Rarely does one actually have two bosses, but it is not uncommon for an individual to be placed in a situation when two persons higher up in the organization place different sets of expectations on him. And as the saying goes, no man can successfully please two masters.

At first brush, one may not realize that this is a problem for policemen. As mentioned earlier, police departments are often highly structured organizations with specific and formal communication channels clearly identified. One would generally not expect policemen to experience conflicting demands. Nevertheless, job conflict is a significant stressor for policemen. For example, conflict arises between what the "top brass" expects and what the immediate supervisor expects. Further there is what can only be called a schizophrenic situation that often exists between city hall and the police department. City hall has its own ideas of what a policeman should do, and the police chief has other ideas. Both sets of expectations are communicated to the police officer. (The split usually arises over the function of "police officer as community servant running any errand that the city deems necessary" and "police officer as a crime-fighting specialist.") This confused split occurs throughout the chain of command and causes various senior officers to put their own (and often differing expectations) onto the next lower level of command.

Thus, the poor officer at the bottom of this chain-of-command may find himself in the situation of one policeman, who, reflecting on this problem, stated that, "At one time, the officer may be told by supervisors to enforce laws a certain way because of political pressures on the police administration and then later, be told exactly the opposite."

Another problem (conflict) arises when an officer tries to enforce a law and hooks a political figurehead rather than just an ordinary unknown citizen. The pressure brought to bear on the officer can be immense, resulting in job transfer and even, on occasion, ruining of his career. So, job conflict is heightened, and the officer becomes confused as to when certain people are considered "hands off" as far as arrests and citations are concerned.

Not only tagging a politician, but also ticketing his friends can be frought with hidden danger. As reported by J. Gardiner (1970), "One Massachusetts legislator, invited by a local League of Woman Voters to discuss the function of a legislator, startled the ladies by beginning, 'The chief function of a legislator is to fix traffic tickets for his constituents.' " It is not difficult to believe that such events have far-reaching effects on the police officer.

The job conflict problem of discordant expectations is further expanded for the average cop on the street by the additional divergence of expectations placed on him by the many "significant others" or what some call "police audiences," e.g. friends, family, judges, lawyers, businessmen, civil rights leaders, other police, politicians, newspaper men, and John Q. Public, in general, in his life. All make their demands and so create a state of conflict in the police officer.

James W. Sterling (1972) in his book, *Changes in Role Concepts of Police Officers,* gives an interesting example of how this role conflict can occur in dealing with police audiences in "just one small part of his role" as police officer.

> In Bob's department, there was a general order which required that, "patrolmen check doors and windows in stores and businesses at irregular time intervals during evening hours." The chief wanted this done—so the trainers told the recruit. When Bob got in the field, he was told by his supervisor that he should check doors and windows—but it's unnecessary when the business is checked by a private watch service.
>
> Later, when Bob began to talk to more experienced patrolmen, they told him that, "it's a waste of time to do these security checks." They suggested that he might shake a few doorknobs when a supervisor is around or there are citizens on the street—but that's all. The exception would be the merchant who was willing to pay a few dollars to a patrolman for a little extra attention to his building.
>
> Contrary to what he had been told in the field, our recruit knew from reading his role model's book, *Police Administration,* by O. W. Wilson, the patrolmen should check the security of doors and windows of commercial buildings even when private watch services were utilized.
>
> Because of a rise in commercial burglaries, the Chamber of Commerce expressed its strong opinion in a newspaper article that doors and windows should be checked by police patrolmen frequently and regularly whenever a business is closed—including the daylight hours on Sundays.
>
> A community group of residents later reacted to the statement of the Chamber of Commerce and publicly voiced its opinion that the police should not perform security checks at all. In its view, the police should concentrate their patrol effort in residential areas—protecting citizens, not buildings. They added that businessmen should pay for private watchman service and not burden the police with it.
>
> A spokesman for the Association of Private Watchmen concurred with the community group and stated that the police should not be in the watchman business.

Another aspect of job conflict for the cop is the stress of having to get along with people. Like the receptionist, sales clerk, public relations specialist, complaints department representative, salesman, or other public man, the police officer is required to maintain a polite, civil manner, even though inside he may be disgusted with an obnoxious individual who is provoking him. Police have to deal with people when they are both threatening and vulnerable, when they are angry, when they are frightened, when they are desperate, and when they are drunk and violent. And through all this, the policeman is supposed to remain cool. Again the pressures on the police officer are more extreme than those of other workers who also have this problem to face. Few others have to deal with such extremes as loud drunks, child beaters, pimps, people with chips on their shoulders or people who hate cops to the point of obsession. Being nice under these conditions is a most difficult task for the police officer and can produce acute strain reactions within him.

Another conflict arises frequently when a police officer must enforce laws that he may personally question (a conflict in value judgment). As an example, for some, marijuana is not considered to be a vice or social problem, however, officers must make public arrests. There are other less controversial laws appearing on the books that the policeman privately questions but must publicly enforce, such as the question of the "victimless" crimes of gambling or prostitution. Not only may the officer privately question the specific statute's worth but he is also frustrated by having to spend time on these cases instead of on cases he considers to be more serious.

Issuing parking tickets is such a situation. A policeman may not feel it is part of his job as a crime fighter to write parking tickets. Yet he is faced with the fact that to advance on his job he must write at least some parking tags. Many officers, thus, become trapped; they personally do not feel writing a parking or speeding ticket (especially if the offender is only going a few miles over the limit) or fining a citizen for a violation such as not curbing his dog is important or even right, but they are required to do so. As one New York cop said to a lady as he wrote out a ticket for her not picking up her dog's deposit on the street, "I personally don't want to give you this, but my chief is over there looking."

Complicating this problem is the fact that there are laws on the books that the cop is required to enforce but which the public wishes he would discretely ignore. Such is the case with the "blue laws" in effect in several states.

Consider also gambling, *re:* private poker parties. The officer may personally feel that each citizen has the right to choose how he conducts himself as long as he is not harming anyone else. The policeman is put in an awkward position, however, when he puts on his badge and has to act according to the law and go out and arrest participants in a private poker party. The officer is forced to punish people he personally feels should not be punished.

A final difficulty within this stressor is the officer's potential conflict over being required to work in assignments, such as a desk job, when his preferred assignment is out on the streets "where the action is." You can imagine the immediate effect this has when an active policeman, who enjoys action, is transferred to a sedentary desk job. As the police locker room comment goes about the cop so transferred, "Yes, I knew him. He used to work for the police department." Such also is the case with those officers who work a beat mainly servicing the affluent. These officer's primary problems are dog bites, brush fires, and criminal damage reports. And as one officer comments, "The people, generally, have the attitude that they're better than average, and treat you as their servant." Few active, self-respecting policemen desire such assignments. Such incidents portray the conflict that develops when there is discrepancy between what an officer wants to do and what he is required to do.

Second Job

Another potential stressor that the police profession has in common with other occupations is moonlighting. Though anyone can potentially moonlight and hold down an additional part-time job, most workers find it difficult to do so. The outstanding exceptions are firemen, medical doctors, lawyers, and other degreed professionals, and policemen.

There are a number of opportunities for extra work for police. For one, like firemen, many policemen work a shift schedule that allows them time during the day to take on another job.

Also, many local businesses need police assistance on a part-time basis for activities, such as directing traffic in and out of their parking lots, keeping the peace, and providing extra security protection. Not only is there a source of part-time work available which the police officer is uniquely qualified to perform, but the policeman is often sought out and encouraged to take on extra jobs by these community businessmen. Even within the police department there are chances for overtime work. Police departments are generally understaffed and consistently have manpower shortages. The main avenue available to overcome this deficit is to create overtime opportunities for members of the force. And so, as a result of both the availability of overtime within the police department and outside job opportunities, many officers work more than the usual forty-hour week.

It needs to be emphasized that moonlighting or overtime work is not necessarily always a stressor. However, it becomes a stressor when it creates fatigue which is carried over into one's primary job. It also can become a stressor for policemen's wives, as the following comments by a police officer's wife shows.

My first and foremost concern is my husband's health and happiness. When a man, whether he is a policeman or just an everyday office worker, works two jobs, the stress is very great, but a police officer has a greater stress because in the type of job he does, he may be called upon at any given moment to save a life, arrest a burglar, or any number of things. If he hasn't had the proper rest or if he is so fatigued that he cannot think straight, it may cost him his life, the life of a fellow officer, or an innocent bystander.

The second and also a very important factor is family life. My husband is not now, but has in the past worked a second job, and the change in him is very definite. When he is getting the proper rest and food, he is a loving, giving father to our two boys and loving husband. He has the time to listen to problems they may have and go to little league games.

Our home life is usually pretty smooth running and uncomplicated, the opposite is true when he is working a second job. In just a few days he has turned into a crabby individual, who has no time for anything except work. He doesn't eat right or sleep right, he is very nervous, tired, listless and constantly on the run. He gets up goes to work at his first job, works eight hours, comes home changes clothes grabs a bite to eat, rests a few minutes, then leaves for his second job.

Another wife, depressed over her husband's many hours away from home on the first and second job, succinctly states, "I get tired of being home alone, of being both a mother and father."

Digressing for a moment, we tend to forget how great a part of our day is spent in work-related activities. Consider an average worker; he needs an hour in the morning to eat breakfast and get ready for work, another half hour for getting to work, eight hours at work with an additional half hour set aside for lunch, another half hour to get home, and at least another hour to unwind and have dinner. Only 13½ hours are left. Take eight hours out for sleep, and this leaves only 5½ hours per day available for a second job during the week. Is it really any wonder that the male worker becomes the zombie at home that the average American housewife complains about? Exhausted from work, the only time he has to catch up, providing he is not working a second weekday job, is the evening hours; the time his wife wants companionship and family activity.

The job of policing is quite exhausting, and a police officer needs the full 5½ hours a day to rest and recuperate. The extra job can only cut into this time or the time set aside for sleep, unless the second job is done only on weekends. The extra job, then, can only act to fatigue him and create a spillover effect onto his main job. The response capability of the officer who works overtime or holds down a second job will be lowered, his needed split-second alertness may not be there, and so he will be less able to cope with the crises and stressors in his regular police work. To borrow a term from Hans Selye, the policeman's "adaptation energy" is reduced, and thus he is more likely to become a candidate for an accident or physical or mental health problem.

Like a policeman, some of us can hold down a second job, and those of us who do, share this potential stress. But unlike the policeman, the rest of us can coast on our main job (at least for awhile, until our energy level is renewed) because we are not required, as the policeman is, to be constantly at a state of peak preparedness.

Inactivity

Another stressor, common to several occupations is the stressor of inactivity. The stress researcher has a technical term for this problem, job underload. Job underload may be both qualitative and quantitative. Qualitative job underload refers to boring, repetitive work such as that done by auto workers on the Detroit assembly lines. On an assembly line the worker is physically active but, in many cases, mentally understimulated and thus bored. Quantitative job underload, on the other hand refers to the boredom arising from physical inactivity; the idleness that arises from having little to do on the job.

In policing, both difficulties are common. A policeman may be on call, e.g. on a stakeout waiting for something to happen, or he may be repetitively active, e.g. operating a radar unit or writing out citations or cruising empty streets eight hours a day. During the "graveyard" shift the streets are often quiet, and there is nothing to do. The research of Daniel Cruse and Jessie Rubin who undertook an in-depth study of twelve radio patrol car officers illuminates the problems. Rubin (1972) summarizes as follows:

> . . . much of the time is taken up simply in cruising over and over again through an assigned zone of the city. Our study shows that the average number of police-citizen contacts on an eight-hour shift is 4.4 Though we did not time the duration of contacts, it is unlikely that they averaged an hour each; but even if they did average an hour, then 3.6 hours of each eight-hour shift (about 43% of the time) is taken up with simply cruising. That is a conservative estimate.
>
> As a result, the patrolman, particularly at night, is subjected to severe boredom and lack of sensory stimulation. Policemen have a number of ways of coping with this. Some of them periodically get out of their assigned zone and race along for a few minutes on a super-highway. Some, I have been told (but for obvious reasons did not observe) , look for women and engage in sexual intercourse. Some sleep. If one isn't in a two-man car with a partner to talk to, other more common devices for combatting boredom are stopping to chat with other patrolmen or backing up a neighboring patrol car sent on a call. Some policemen endeavor to "look for action" by self-initiated police-citizen contacts and investigations. In our study, the frequency of police-citizen contacts initiated by patrolmen was at its peak from 2:00 to 4:00 A.M., when boredom and sensory deprivation were at their most intense.

A most interesting finding of the Cruse-Rubin research (1973) is that fatigue "does not contribute much to deteriorated police performance with an important exception . . . increase in fatigue on the job is most closely related to shifts where *little* activity occurs. Fatigue thus seems to be largely a product of inactivity."

The above discussion centers on boredom of the patrol car officer. What about the cop who walks a beat? James Ahern (1972), expolice chief of New Haven, Connecticut discusses in the following passage the street policeman's boredom:

> The walking cop usually alternates hours standing on a corner and walking a predetermined and precisely timed route. While he stands on his corner, departmental regulations are likely to dictate to him which particular square of concrete he will occupy . . . During this hour, if he walks down the street to exercise his legs, to look in a store window, or to talk to a friend, he must make up an excuse for the sergeant, whose sole job it is to check on his position.
>
> Anyone with a moderate degree of intelligence and the slightest bit of energy will go insane standing on the same street corner for an hour at a time. Occasional passers-by who ask the cop for directions offer him little stimulation. Once a week there may be an auto accident nearby, or a store owner may complain of shoplifting, or the cop may come upon someone peddling merchandise without a license. But these things happen so seldom . . .
>
> The walking beat is stultifying on the day and swing shifts; it is impossible on the midnight shift. Here the policeman is strictly a night watchman. When he is not standing on his corner, he is trudging up and down streets trying doors and checking windows to make sure they are all locked . . .

There is a public misconception that criminals come out at night (as the devils and demons of past centuries were supposed to do), and that the night is, therefore the busiest time for the police. The potential felon, like the rest of us, does not enjoy being out on the streets when it is dark. This is especially true in winter, in those climates where the freezing temperatures make it uncomfortable to be outside. Thus in the wee hours of the morning, a policeman's activity often is minimal.

It comes as a surprise to most of us, once we go beyond the TV image of the cop, to find out that a great deal of police work is simply routine and boring. As one police psychiatrist states, "So here you have a job that's one of the most demanding there is, and yet filled with the sheerest drudgery imaginable." When the author first became involved in studying the police, it was amazing to see how eagerly many policemen looked forward to dangerous situations. This was before the power of the stressor of inactivity/ boredom was understood. It is the crises that serve as escape valves and allow the officer adventure and excitement.

Private reports from policemen, as well as documented research, have shown that the need for action to avoid boredom is so great that policemen occasionally engage in marginal activities such as arresting or baiting drunks or hippies just to have something to do. It is well known that the human organism has an optimal level of arousal, and that too little stimulation is as harmful, and as much of a stressor, as too much stimulation. Such is the case of inactivity.

It is also true, of course, that the stressor of inactivity is most difficult on the individual who works alone. Inactivity is considered by some to be one of the main stressors on firemen, as they sit around the firehouse for hours on end with nothing to do. Yet, in reality, the effects are mitigated because they are facing this stressor in a group and together while away the time. The policeman, however, is often alone. This isolation added to the mental and/or physical understimulation increases the overall effect of this stressor.

Job Overload

Job overload, as the name implies, is just the opposite of job underload. Here there is either too much to do, or the individual is given a task which is too difficult to perform. Technically, as in job underload, the two components of overload can be labelled, respectively, quantitative and qualitative overload. A person is said to be experiencing quantitative overload when he has too much to do, and qualitative job overload when demands are made which are beyond his ability to fulfill. In the former case the individual has the skills to perform the necessary tasks, he just does not have the time to get them all done. In the latter case no matter how much time the individual is given, he does not have the necessary skills to perform the tasks at acceptable levels.

Qualitative job overload occurs in policing because expectations are placed on the officer by society (and even his department) which, in reality, no individual can meet. The officer is expected to have the knowledge of a person with a combined MD, PhD, LLB, MSW, SJ, and be a diligent blue-collar worker besides. As George Kirkham (1974), professor turned cop states,

> As a police officer myself, I found that society demands too much of its policemen. Not only are they expected to enforce the law, they must also be curbside psychiatrists, marriage counselors, social workers— even ministers and doctors. I found that a good street officer combines in his daily work splinters of each one of these complex professions, and many more. It is unreasonable, of course, to ask so much of the men in blue; nevertheless, there is no one else to whom a person can turn for help in the kind of crises and problems with which policemen must deal.

To give one a better idea of the overload on a policeman's job, the following is an excerpt taken from one city's ordinance defining the duties of a police officer:

> GENERAL STATEMENT OF DUTIES: Performs general police duty in the protection of life and property through the enforcement of laws and ordinances; does related work as required.
> DISTINGUISHING FEATURES OF THE CLASS: This is general duty police work consisting of routine patrol in an assigned area, preliminary investigation, and miscellaneous duties incidental thereto, performed in accordance with departmental rules and regulations. A senior officer regularly checks the work and gives specific instructions and assistance when special problems arise; however, an officer is required to exercise initiative and discretion when faced with emergency conditions. The work involves an element of personal danger and the occasional performance of hazardous tasks under emergency conditions.
> EXAMPLES OF WORK: (Illustrative only) Enforces the laws and ordinances of the city and all other pertinent laws; Patrols an assigned area during a specific period; Checks doors and windows and examines premises of unoccupied buildings or residences in order to detect any suspicious conditions; Investigates suspicious conditions and complaints, and makes arrests of persons who violate laws and ordinances; Accompanies prisoners to headquarters, jail or court and appears in court as arresting officer; Directs traffic and either arrests or gives violation tickets to those who break traffic laws; Checks automobile parking in restricted areas and gives violation tickets when necessary; Responds to accidents, giving all possible assistance and preparing necessary

reports; Maintains order in crowds and attends parades, funerals or other public gatherings; Watches for stolen cars and wanted or missing persons; Makes investigations and enforces city and state laws pertaining to juvenile offenders; Answers criminal complaints and takes necessary corrective action; Gives advice on laws, ordinances, and general information to the public; Oversees custody and care of prisoners when assigned to such duty; Give emergency first-aid treatment to injured persons; Maintains records and prepares reports; Lifts fingerprints from crime scene, takes photographs and otherwise compiles evidence; Takes fingerprints of suspects and others for the use of the department or for other govermental use; Attends professional training sessions as scheduled.

The effect of this overload should be obvious. In an informal survey of officers in the city mentioned above, over 70 percent of the officers felt they were under the stress of job overload. As further reported by the officer who conducted the survey:

> The present department consists of 21 men, over half are under 35 years of age and their health is, for the most part, excellent. But what about the older men with more experience, how is their health? There has been two nervous breakdowns, one heart attack, several ulcers and one case of high blood pressure. All but three or four officers smoke to excess. Three officers are having serious marriage difficulties with one divorce.

As if the job overload for this department is not already enough, this city (like a growing number of other small towns) recently has gone over to the public safety officer concept. Here, in addition to the regular duties of a police officer, the public safety officer is required to: respond to fire calls and extinguish fires, operate fire apparatus and equipment, participate in periodic fire drills and training sessions, and make occasional fire inspections and assist with fire prevention activities. Thus, an already overloaded police force will become even more so.

Quantitative overload, of course, varies considerably from police force to police force and even varies considerably within a police department, depending on the assignment or district patrolled. For example in a densely populated area, such as an inner-city ghetto, there are too many tasks for the individual officer to perform. The officer may be in a constant state of overload. In other assignments in the same city or in less "over-

whelmed" cities, overload may be cyclical in nature, so that there
will be peak periods when this stress is in evidence followed by
long stretches of calm. However, as the President's Commission
on Law Enforcement and Administration of Justice (1967)
found, "In practically every department, the caseloads carried
by detectives are too heavy to allow them to follow through
thoroughly on more than a small percentage of cases assigned
to them." Thus, though the overload may vary, for most officers
it is still too much.

The problem of case overload is often complicated for the
detective because of the public's image of the police. The public
views the policeman as the "Kojak" type or the "Streets of San
Francisco" cop. Looking into a real policeman's job is not like
viewing a television story. The same results cannot be met in
reality, as on the television, due to the frustrations that develop
through inadequate equipment, the overload of paperwork, and
an understaffed police department. The citizens often expect the
impossible with the use of scientific equipment that only exists
in the fantansy world of television and movies.

There is one other aspect of job overload that is significant for
policemen, that is what may be called environmental complexification. This refers to the rate at which one's environment becomes
complex. When the rate exceeds the individual's ability to adjust,
breakdown occurs. Such is the case when an individual from a
small village goes to live in the big city. It has been shown in
policing, for example, that the police recruit who has the most
difficult time adjusting is the one who comes from a rural town to
work as a city policeman. Even the "sophisticated" city dweller
may become overwhelmed with the rapid pace of life and the
barrage of changing events, conditions, and life styles.

Environmental complexification is certainly a factor that affects
policemen. As part of his job, an officer must deal with the changing mores of our society, values that change much faster than
the laws he must enforce. The cop must become familiar with
a maze of rules and ordinances which are continually being re-
interpreted by our court system. In general, the cop is the first
one to face the conflict that arises from any change in our complex society. For example, heroin usage probably arose with the

necessity of frustrated inner-city dwellers to escape. But, however it started, the police were the first to feel the effects of its increased usage, for they were the ones who had to deal with the resulting increase in crime. Or as an even more recent example, segments of society are experimenting with the right to public nudity, such as on the nude beaches on the west coast. The police are the first elements of the traditional society brought in to stop and arrest these new "change agents." But there are differing philosophical values involved here and the policeman, as with the rest of us, is often not prepared to deal with them, yet, unlike us, he is required to act definitively.

It should be noted that under conditions of overload individual workers tend to respond in ways which are less than optimum, such as incorrectly processing information, failing to process some of the information, or even running away from the overload situation. Any one of these responses can have dire consequences for law enforcement.

Shift Work

> . . . the human adult is an animal whose body is tuned by evolution and training to go about its business during the hours of daylight and sleep during those of darkness. Ask it to work at night and sleep during the day and it does both rather badly (Wilkinson, 1970).

This eloquent quote refers to a stressor shared by all too many occupations; that is shift work. The roots of the problems associated with shift work lie in the difficulty people have adapting their physiological and psychological rhythms to a new and unfamiliar sleep-wakefulness cycle. The problem of shift work is a complicated one, and to understand the effects of this stressor on the individual both physical and psychological components must be discussed, as the total effect on the individual is a product of the interaction of these two components.

Physiologically, many of our bodily processes fluctuate according to a cyclical rhythm (see Fig. 6). The twenty-four-hour cyclical rhythm has been given the technical name circadian rhythm. If the cycle follows the twenty-four-hour day/night pattern, it may also be called a diurnal rhythm. Circadian rhythms are seen in

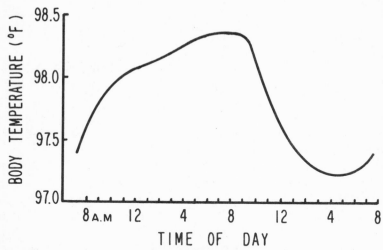

Figure   6. Relationship of body temperature to time of day.

fluctuations of body temperature; urine flow; renal excretion of sodium, potassium, and phosphates; metabolism; heart rate; skin conductance; cortical and medullary production of adrenal hormones; sleep cycle; and general mental and physical functioning. In fact, researchers have found that practically all physiological functions show circadian rhythm cycles. Shift work will come in conflict with these circadian rhythms. The resulting negative effect on the individual (if any), however, will depend on a number of other factors. Of extreme importance among these factors is the social-psychological environment within which the shift work occurs.

Our society is based on a daytime schedule. We go to work during the day, eat during the day, shop during the day; in fact, almost all communal activities are daytime activities. Those few that are not, usually end by early evening. Even the late nighttime bars typically close at 2:00 A.M. Our society has built up a daytime social system and we, as individuals, have become accustomed to it. To ask a person to deviate by working the late night (graveyard) shift means asking him to cut himself off from the normal avenues of social interaction. If you are a single fellow, imagine yourself asking for a date and then telling your would be companion that you will pick her up at 5:00 A.M. when you get off work. The havoc is even greater if the shift worker is a family man. The shift worker's wife must maintain two households, the normal daytime schedule for herself and the children and a separate schedule for her husband. This is quite taxing on her as she must prepare separate meal schedules, co-ordinate separate sleeping schedules, try to keep the children from making too much noise during the day when her husband is asleep, jumping to answer the phone on the first ring so as not to disturb her sleeping husband, and so on. Further she must often be alone at night, a condition which can be quite un-settling for many women.

The shift worker does not get to see as much of his children as he would like to (consider the plight of the officer on second shift, 3:00 P.M. to 1:00 A.M.: during the school year, weekends are the only time he may be together with his children); he is limited to visiting stores and entertainment centers as they are closed when he gets off work; and it is difficult for him to parti-cipate in organized social activities. Few neighbors would accept a bridge party invitation for 4:00 A.M. or even 9:00 A.M.

If the shift schedule extends over a long period of time, there will be some degree of physiological adaptation, so that many of the biological rhythms will adjust to the new schedule. Un-fortunately, for most police departments the permanent night shift schedule is a rare entity, and the changing shift pattern predominates. To my knowledge the most extensive pattern in policing is the twenty-eight-day or monthly shift schedule (though some departments rotate as often as every week). One may think of a twenty-eight-day routine as a long period of time, plenty of time to adjust (at least physiologically), but this is deceptive. In actuality the worker is on a 5/2 schedule, as on the weekend he often reverts to a daytime schedule to fit in with his family and the rest of society.

With a changing or rotating shift schedule the problems as-sociated with physiological adaptation increase. It takes several days for the average individual to readjust his eating and sleeping habits. For many, no sooner do they adjust, then they are forced to change gears and go on a different shift. The extent of this problem can be gleaned from a study we did several years ago. In this study, ninety-three out of one hundred police officers surveyed mentioned disruption of eating habits as a problem resulting from changing shift routines. Over 30 percent of the same officers also mentioned disruption of sleep habits as a problem. Interestingly, one major city police department adopted a weekly shift schedule, which was formalized into law, to protect patrolmen from the arbitrary use of power on the part of supervisors, who were putting officers on the less desirable shifts as a form of punishment. Unfortunately, to avoid one problem the department probably created a bigger one, and as one would expect, with the short shift cycle, the problem of sleep adjustment for officers was intensified. In that city, exposés in the local papers of policemen caught sleeping in their cars can be found. Of course the officers are punished, but such behavior must be expected of a sleep-deprived individual whose daytime sleep is not adequate or satisfying.

It should be noted that, daytime sleep in the controlled laboratory has been found to be qualitatively different from nighttime sleep and less satisfying. Further, in the home, daytime noises (of children, traffic, etc.) make prolonged sleeping more difficult, even if there were no noticable physiological differences. Add to this adjustment problems arising from changing sleep patterns due to rotating shifts and you, indeed, have fitful sleep.

One additional problem that arises because of shift work is the problem of unwinding after work. If a patrolman, for example gets off work at three in the morning, it is unlikely that he can go home, relax, have a drink and sit and chat with his wife, because his wife and children are fast asleep. Yet he still needs to unwind, and unfortunately at that hour, the only place to unwind is the all-night bar. And there, if he meets an attentive female stranger, he may create more problems than he went to release. (Some police departments have been rather creative in handling this difficulty. For example, one department operates an all-night bowling alley for the policemen, so they have an alternative place to go. One officer's creative, yet at the same time sad solution to the problem was to ride around with personnel from the next shift schedule until he unwound enough to go home and sleep.)

Because of the intensity of individual and family adjustment problems, shift work may be considered one of the most potent stressors for the police profession. Although there are some individuals who thrive on late work, i.e. who enjoy the quietness, the reduction of the number of interfering supervisors, etc., for many changing shift routines are quite damaging, both physiologically and psychologically. In fact, in surveys of why individuals leave the police department, the inability to cope with the problems associated with shift routines always looms high.

The tragedy of this problem cannot be truly understood until one listens to individual cases. The author maintains a small clinical practice and over the years has seen clients who evidence marital difficulties and/or have problem children whose difficulties can be traced directly to problems arising out of the effects of shift work on the family. Further, in lecturing on the problems of shift work, students occasionally come to me after class to relate that their fathers were shift workers and they intimate that they missed their fathers while growing up and felt cheated. Often they feel as if they had to shoulder many of the responsibilities their fathers should have carried. They then recount the resulting difficulties this caused because they were not equipped to assume such adult burdens. Indeed, shift work is a major, though hidden, factor in the etiology of psychological adjustment problems for many individuals.

Inadequate Resources

This stressor arises from the inability of a worker to control decisions affecting his job or from the lack of availability of proper materials, work space, etc. to perform his job properly.

Lack of voice in decision making is a problem we have touched on already. But previously it was mentioned in terms of the frustration the police officer feels as a result of his being treated more like a child than as a trained professional. Here, however, the lack of say refers more to its consequences in terms of the policeman's ability to adequately carry out his job. It is maddening for all of us in our jobs when we see some improvement that could be made, or know the best way to get something done yet be unable to present this information to the organization, which prefers to perpetuate the SOP (standard operating procedure). Like the factory worker who sees how to improve the assembly process he works on, the tool and die maker who finds the errors in the engineer's blueprint, or the construction foreman who realizes that the construction design is faulty, the police officer has learned to keep quiet. However, unlike these other workers, the policeman realizes that the inefficiencies he must put up with seriously affect the lives of others. Lack of adequate equipment can reduce his ability to deter crime and increase the likelihood of the tragedy of more victims of violence. Knowing this, wanting to act, and being unable to do anything about it, naturally, leads to the development of frustration.

The problem of lack of proper equipment and material is definitely a stressor shared with other professions. For many of us, support services are in short supply or even lacking, and, as a result, we fail to get the needed backup, be it inadequate staff support, lack of appropriate laboratory equipment, inadequate or slow clerical aid, or delay in receiving needed materials. In terms of clerical support, the police officer often must act as his own secretary, painstakingly filling out form after form. Besides lack of support, lack of equipment also plagues the policeman. As one officer put it, "It is bothersome to find that when another policeman gets hurt, that it could have been prevented with proper equipment." Further, the shortage of police manpower and high crime rate make it such that the officer is "stretched thin" covering a wide territory, with inadequate manpower backup.

The problem of equipment was aptly described by Robert Daly in his book, *Target Blue* (1971). As Daly explains, the New York City police department, employing over 43,000 officers, had only *one* electronic transmitting device known as a body set. This device allows backup police to monitor conversation when an officer (usually an undercover cop) goes into a risky situation. Because there was only one set, when an officer finished what may have been a harrowing and tiring experience, the officer had to return the device (so that it was available for others, if an emergency arose) before quitting for the day (or night).

The following comment by an experienced officer, further illuminate this difficulty:

> When the officer is charged with certain responsibilities, and then not backed up with equipment there is conflict—the lack of the spotlights in police vehicles is a good example. Due to this lack of a simple piece of equipment the officer cannot adequately check business at night against burglary without spending three to ten times longer. Time he does not have. Thus burglaries increase, the result: supervisors are unhappy, and the officer is called on the carpet for allowing it to occur, told to work harder, and not let it happen again. Yet, he still does not have the spotlight!

Inadequate resources also increase the work load. If the equipment and personnel are not available the officer is required to either work overtime hours to make up for the deficiency or rush through his case load to make time for the extra work.

Some argue (in a somewhat tongue-in-cheek manner) that inadequate resources is not a stressor but a *frustrator*. As one officer, holding this view, stated, "It is frustrating to have to stand for 20 minutes (at a scene of a minor accident) and wait for the life squad, unable to perform a service, unable to carry out a charge you feel you were given, because there are no splints in your car." This lack of equipment was a frustrator to this and many other officers.

Inequities in Pay or Job Status

This stressor refers to the problem of being paid too little for one's work or having too low a status job for the level of one's responsibility or quality of work performance. Dissatisfaction with pay is a common complaint for most of us. The question is the degree of this dissatisfaction; is it something we just gripe about or does it go deeper? Policemen, in general, do not fare too well on this problem. For instance, in a recent study we found that in comparison with twenty-three other stressed occupations, the police showed the *greatest* degree of dissatisfaction with their pay. In the Watson and Sterling (1969) survey, in answer to the question, "What is the most important problem you as an individual face?" Fifty-seven percent of the officers checked the alternative "not enough pay." (As an aside, the second highest alternative checked was, "little respect shown by others for my profession.")

An example of the problem of pay can be gleaned from the following report (taken from the *Police Reporter,* May 20, 1974).

Georgia Finds Low Pay Key Factor in Police Turnover

Personnel turnover in Atlanta-area police departments averaged almost 30% in 1971, according to a report issued by the Atlanta Regional Commission, and in some communities the rate reached 90%. The report blames low salaries as a major factor and says that at least half of the 27 communities in its survey said they had trouble recruiting applicants. In a separate study, the Georgia State Crime Commission reported that about half the men who left metro area police departments during a three-year-period gave pay dissatisfaction as the reason for quitting. Discussing the effect on police families, a spokesman for the Commission said, "It's particularly tough on the kids and hard when a policeman has to moonlight to make ends meet." One local department that had a 90% turnover in 1971 gave its men a 25% increase fifteen months ago. Since then only one member has resigned.

The key to understanding why the policeman's dissatisfaction is so high lies in the definition of this stressor, "being paid too little *for one's work.*" The policeman not only works hard, but at times actually puts his life on the line. In return for giving so much of himself, the policeman expects appropriate financial reward. Aside from working hard and working under dangerous conditions, the policeman has developed special skills that leads him to feel that he should be paid as a professional, rather than as a blue-collar worker. Think for a moment about what is required of a policeman. At a minimum, to do his job properly, he must in part be a social worker, public relations expert, crowd control specialist, priest, lawyer, medic, crisis prevention expert, such as preventing suicides, criminology specialist, psychologist, weapons expert, trained fighter, responsible executive (in terms of being required to make decisions which have enormous consequences), be physically fit, have a keen memory for detail and events (which the officer needs not only to stop crime but to successfully testify in a court room), and even develop special visual alertness skills.

As an example of the special skills required to be a policeman let us consider special visual alertness. One of the first times the author rode in a squad car, he was surprised to find out that the police officer was able to remember license plate numbers at a great distance and with a short time exposure. Even upon concerted effort and repeated attempts, the author could not come close to matching the officer's ability in this area.

The second part of this stressor, inequity in job status, may even be more difficult for the policeman to cope with. It is hard for him to accept the low job status of his position considering the many highly-skilled activities he undertakes. Just to give one illustration, psychiatrists usually work from 9:00 A.M. to 4:00 P.M. and have high paying jobs and social status. When the psychiatrist "closes up shop" for the day, the policeman in most cities becomes the only health care agent available during the late evening and early morning hours. (Who else will counsel a family with problems at 4:00 A.M.?) The policeman may even have a greater case load and show more dramatic successes, such as in suicide prevention, than his fellow professional the psychiatrist. But in job status instead of being similar to the psychiatrist, the police officer ranks more closely with the garbage collector. And even worse his low job status is often a consequence of the view that police officers are dumb, and sometimes brutal and unfit company for self-respecting people.

The problem of low status is further magnified for police officers by having it constantly brought to their attention. Other professions may be considered to be low in status, but the workers in them are not continually being made aware of their low status. The police, however, almost daily are faced with situations on and off the job which bring their inequity in status directly to their attention (see Chap. 3, specifically the section on Negative Public Relations, for an elaboration of this point). Bluntly put, policing is not a high status profession.

Organizational Territoriality

Robert Ardrey's armchair excursion into the world of the Territorial Imperative has brought to our and perhaps to other readers' attentions the potential importance which personal space and territory may play in the everyday activities of man. To what extent is territory important to people in modern organizations? Do people develop a feeling of ownership with respect to their own offices or their own departments? Shouldn't the time a person spends in other territories prove to be a source of stress for the individual? What types of strains, such as insecurity, do people show when they cross the boundary between their own section of the organization and other sections—or move out from their own organization completely (as the salesman does as an everyday part of his job)? Indeed, every time a person moves out of his territory, he invades the territory of someone else, potentially putting the other person as well as himself under stress (French and Caplan, 1973).

This excerpt brings into focus the next stressor policemen share with some other occupations, the problem of working in organizationally alien territory. French and Caplan, studying the impact of this stressor on engineers working in an administrative unit and conversely administrators working in an engineering unit, concluded that organizational territoriality is indeed a relevant stressor for the modern world. They found that men working in alien environments experienced stress and concluded that, "crossing an organizational boundary and working in an alien territory entails stress and strain and poses a threat to one's health."

Before discussing the relevance of this stressor to police, it might be helpful to elaborate on one term mentioned in the above quote, the term *personal space*. An easy way for the reader to evaluate the importance of an individual's personal space is to undertake the following experiment. When someone else is talking to you, note the physical distance between you. Then move in closer to the person you are conversing with. At some point you will violate this individual's personal space; he will become uncomfortable, and, in turn, will move away from you. An objective viewer will see that at the closest there was several feet between the two of you, plenty of room, so there was no "objective" need to move apart. The other individual's retreat is tapping some underlying mechanism which is postulated as the need for personal territory or space.

This territorial imperative appears to occur not only for the individual and his personal space, but also for the larger social units the individual is a part of, such as his family and home territory, and of importance from the perspective of job stress, the territoriality that develops on the job.*

Job territoriality with accompanying feelings of possessiveness and comfort seems to develop around those parts of the organiza-

---

*To show that territoriality is a powerful phenomenon, note an individual home owner's strong feeling over his right of property, and his reaction when an alien trespasses, be the trespass ever so harmless, such as someone just cutting across the yard, or turning his car around in the owner's driveway.

tion and/or work environment that one has learned to treat as familiar. The areas in which one has his most frequent job-related interactions and the people he most commonly deals with become the familiar and part of the home territory; what is left is the alien territory. And as in the days of old, there is a buildup of anxiety and discomfort when one leaves his own territory to do business in the unknown and potentially dangerous alien territory.

Looking now at this stressor as it relates to policing, the problem of organizational territoriality arises from two sources, one within the police department and one external to it.

To help understand the development of this problem within the police department, consider a typical job within policing, that of the patrol car officer. (Though we will examine only one job type for evidence of this stressor in policing, the problem can be found in almost all police assignments.) The patrol car officer typically builds up an established pattern of activities as well as an established group of fellow officers with whom he interacts. Typically, the officer has a set partner, works out of the same district or precinct, and reports to the same boss (or series of bosses). Change any one of these patterns and the patrol car officer enters the realm of the unknown with a commensurate buildup of the stress of territoriality. This can and does happen in several ways: changing the officer's partner, temporarily reassigning him to a new district or division (where he does not know many of the officers), or detailing him to work temporarily in an alien environment, such as on an administrative task at headquarters. Even if the officer stays in the same position, this stressor can hit by his becoming involved with groups within the organization, such as detectives or undercover police, who have a different work setup and even outlook, and with whom he is unfamiliar.

The external aspect of this stressor arises because, like his tribal ancestors, the officer was raised in one subculture with a specific set of values and taboos (see chapter 3, Conflicting Values) and, importantly, trained in one profession with its specific value set. The job of policing forces the officer to interact with people from other job-cultures with different value sets (lawyers, judges, administrators, health officials). Eventually it is hoped that with time the new alien territory and people become familiar and the stress of the unknown decreases. But as the policemen must interact with so many diverse groups and work in diverse cultural settings, making the foreign familiar will be a slow process. And the policeman will have more than enough of this stressor during various stages of his career. Further, there will always be some element of this stress in a police job as he will be continually called upon to enter alien environments in the line of duty.

These situations, both within the department and without, can become stressful to the officer. Whether one is tapping some innate genetic fear, or whether it is just that whenever one deals with the unfamiliar there is a certain aspect of threat or discomfort and anxiety associated with it, we do not know. We do know, however, that whatever the cause, working in alien territory does create stress on the worker.

Responsibility for People

Another potential stressor of policing, that is shared with other job types, relates to responsibility for people. Though the policeman may not have the same degree of responsibility for people as the air traffic controller, (who must make decisions minute by minute that directly affect the physical well being of others), he is frequently required to make decisions that have major consequences for the lives of others. Further, the policeman has a much broader spectrum of responsibility than the air traffic controller. His responsibilities vary from the decision to shoot, to arrest or not, how to counsel a rape victim to ease her emotionality, how to chase an offender if there is risk to innocent bystanders in the area, . . . Also, the guidelines are far more varied and less clear than for the air traffic controller. For example, does the officer take a young offender in or does he let the youth go with just a lecture? His decision will affect the youth for the rest of the youth's life, as the social stigma and criminal record that result will follow and haunt the youth. Even in situations when the decision is clear, the responsibility for others can be agonizing. Trying to keep a potential suicide victim from harming himself, or keeping an individual who has gone temporarily wild from harming others, both require clear action. But the officer knows that his actions are crucial and failure can have tragic consequences. Or, by way of another example, the officer occasionally is called in on an emergency, such as being the first one to arrive at the scene of a serious accident, or to come upon a victim of a brutal assault. The specific action he takes will crucially affect the lives of these people in distress.

Even before a crime occurs, the officer's responsibility for others comes into play since he is likely to be the one who spots potential trouble (a youth who is heading along the wrong life path) before it occurs. Though officially it may not be the officer's responsibility, in actuality he may be the only person who can help. (As with the case of the potential delinquent, typically, the youth's parents and society in general have failed in their job, and the policeman is often the last hope for these children). Contrary to public opinion, there are many good samaritans in police uniform who care and want to do something before it is too late.

An extreme instance of taking over responsibility, when others fail, is presented by James Ahern (1972), who relates the following true experience:

The patrolman soon finds that pettiness and insensitivity pervade most agencies that are supposed to serve the public. He lives with it, but occasionally even the most hard-bitten cop gets involved in a situation that arouses his emotions. Once as a young patrolman I was riding in a squad car with a cop who had a reputation for toughness that at times turned to brutality. We were sent to an apartment house where a baby was reportedly very sick. When we arrived, the baby was choking and gagging, unable to breathe. Without immediate attention it would die. My partner took charge; he scooped up the baby and we took off with red light and siren on the most frightening ride of my life. When we arrived at the hospital, the baby was still breathing but was close to death. With the child in his arms the cop rushed up to a doctor and begged him to save it. But the doctor refused to look at it and ordered him to sit in a waiting room. Desperate, the cop cornered a nurse and screamed at her that the baby was dying. She told him to lay it on a table, and then she left.
The cop tried everything he knew, including mouth-to-mouth respiration. Now, in the halls of the hospital, the baby died in his arms. Enraged and heartbroken, on the verge of tears, he screamed at the doctors and nurses until I thought he would attack them. Fighting my own emotions, I found myself restraining him.

Occurrences like this are not the rule. But the policeman who sees various degrees of neglect all around him can hardly help becoming callous and bitter, and eventually he feels his own sensitivity being destroyed.

This responsibility for the welfare of others can weigh heavily on the police officer who has even a modicum of social consciousness. However, if an officer allowed himself to openly worry about his responsibility for others, he would quickly go to pieces. Thus, it is not too uncommon to find that some police officers will not admit to themselves that they experience this responsibility. They rationalize that what happens to other individuals is a result of their own actions, i.e. it is the criminal who broke the law in the first place, and, thus, must assume the consequences for his own actions. This denial is a surface phenomenon only, a defense against extreme stress. Beneath this adamant exterior, these police officers are concerned and do show the effects of the stress caused by the necessity to be responsible for other people. An additional and related stress often occurs in cases in which officers must make arrests or identify persons as criminals. The policeman realizes that his decision can be the direct cause of a long prison sentence or even a man's death. The police officer is frequently haunted by the possibility that he has been wrong and has unjustly accused someone of committing a crime.

The mental anguish, anxiety, and concern that go along with being responsible for the lives and welfare of people, certainly qualify this as an important job stressor in policing.

Though other stressors may take on significance in individual cases, in general, the ten stressors mentioned in this chapter are the crucial ones for understanding the stressors that police hold in common with other professions. It would be nice if we could stop here. The policeman already has enough pressure from the common stressors mentioned above. Unfortunately, in the "real world" of policing the policeman is not allowed the luxury of having to deal with these stressors alone. That is why the author's nomination for the Academy Award for High Stress Job of the Year goes to policemen, because they have so much more to deal with, as the next chapter will show.

CHAPTER 3 POLICE SPECIFIC STRESSORS

I N THE LAST CHAPTER we looked at some of the stressors that policing has in common with other occupations. Now we will examine those major stressors that are specific to the police profession. There are five of these, namely, courts, negative public image, conflicting values, racial situations, and line of duty/crisis situations.

COURTS

As a policeman myself, I had to struggle on a daily basis through a maze of incredibly and incomprehensibly complex restrictions on how the game of enforcing the law is to be played. And a game I discovered it was indeed, with the odds stacked heavily against the police and society and decidedly in favor of the criminal. I well remember one evening drawing my "Miranda warning" card from my wallet and reading it slowly and carefully to a known narcotics pusher whom we had just arrested with a large quantity of heroin in his possession, fearful that a recitation of it from memory might cause me to omit some word or syllable which might later be transformed by a skilled attorney into a violation of the suspect's "rights." "Lay it on me, baby," he said as he convulsed with laughter halfway through my reading of his rights. Still amused with the degrading spectacle of forcing me to read a statement which I knew by heart from previous arrests, he joined in a word for word recall of his "rights" as I methodically read them off to him. Experiences such as this, which I encountered time and again, led me to the inescapable conclusion that we often allow the law to be turned into a mockery of justice, a tool to be used against society by law violators who are its enemies (Kirkham, 1974).

This quote introduces one of the major stressors unique to the police profession, the problem of courts, the restraints and frustrations placed upon policemen by the American judicial system. The impact of this stressor on the policeman can be gleaned by another comment by Kirkham (the liberal professor who learned reality as a cop).

The toughest adversary a street cop must confront each day is not the armed robber or enraged mob, not the addict, the burglar or the mugger. Rather it is, ironically, the very law which he must struggle against increasingly difficult odds to enforce. It is the smugness and complacency of courts and legislatures, which spin out a hopelessly entangling web of procedural restraints upon men who are charged with the awesome responsibility of protecting our society. This was a bitter discovery, one which the liberal scientist within me had long refused to accept (1974).

Kirkham emphasizes the problem of court rulings and leniency to offenders, however, there is another aspect, just as stressful to police officers, and that is the lack of consideration shown toward the police by the courts. Combined, these two aspects make the problem of courts one of the major psychological stressors for police. To understand why, let us look at the stress a police officer faces in the courtroom. A number of problems are involved: (1) scheduling of the police officer's appearance, (2) lawyer confrontation with the officer, and (3) the attitude of the judge toward the policeman. Following is a brief discussion of each aspect.

As criminal lawyers know, it is a favorite trick to schedule a trial in which a policeman must appear at a time which is inconvenient for the officer, or even to postpone court appearances at the last minute (just to confuse the officer as we shall later see). For example, it is disconcerting to the officer to be called to appear early in the morning on a day when the officer has just gotten off the graveyard shift, exhausted from having put in a full tour of duty. The officer is forced to drive downtown to the court house in heavy rush hour traffic, go through the hassle of finding a place to park (many courts make no provision for special police parking), all the while realizing that he is about to "enter the arena to face the lions."

Though arrived, the officer still has another pretrial frustration awaiting him, the long wait. An officer required to appear for a case which is scheduled on the court docket for 9:00 A.M. may actually wait outside the courtroom for four or more hours before he is called. This long wait occurs because the judge has a heavy load of cases, so to optimize his time, he schedules several cases for one period, such as a morning session, and then goes through the docket, one case after another until he is finished. If the cases take longer than expected the judge then carries over into the afternoon session. Meanwhile our poor defender of the peace is left standing idle till his particular case is called. The above example assumes the officer has only one scheduled court appearance a day. However, it is not uncommon for an officer to be scheduled for criminal court at 9:00 A.M. and traffic court at 1:00 P.M. the same day.

Not only the judge, who has his own job stress problems, but the defense attorney has a gambit that often results in lengthy, frustrating waits for the police officer as the following comment by a cop shows:

> The policeman must appear in court—that is to be expected, but to be kept there at the whim of an attorney is wrong. Many attorneys deliberately absent themselves from the courtroom, feigning appearances at other rooms, just to have the judge delay the proceedings. He does this in hope of discouraging the witnesses, including the policeman from staying in court. When a man has been up all night working and then must sit in court until 1:00, 2:00, or even 3:00 P.M. or more he tends to become disgruntled and the defense attorney knows this and he watches closely to see if the policeman or witnesses leave the courtroom. As soon as he sees the policeman leave, he will rush to the bailiff or clerk and get the case called. With the absence of the policeman the case is dismissed.

The overall unfairness is portrayed in this statement by another cop, "If I do not show up, the case is thrown out of court, no matter what the inconvenience is to me, but if the lawyer wants to go off on a vacation, he just has the case moved back on the docket."

Another major problem is lawyer confrontation. Why should a defense attorney want to confuse or bait the arresting police officer? The answer is simple, it helps his case. If he can discredit the officer he has "scored points" for his defendant with the judge and jury. Thus, the officer is forced to undergo a grilling which makes him squirm. There are several techniques or ways for an attorney to accomplish his goal of discrediting the police officer; all are at the expense of the individual cop. For example, the defense lawyer will play upon the negative image of the policeman and try to portray him as a brutal, sadistic, and unfeeling individual who has it out for the innocent lamb who is the lawyer's client. As one frustrated cop said, "I would like the judge to see the defendant, not in a quiet courtroom setting, but as the street cop sees him beating his small child with a heavy belt buckle, or kicking his pregnant wife. I wish they could see the ravages of crime as the cop on the beat must: innocent people cut, shot, raped, robbed, and murdered. I feel it would give them a different perspective on crime and criminals."

Another tactic is to confront and upset the officer. If the cop can be angered or rattled he will make easier pickings for the defense lawyer and will present a poorer image to the jury. The ordeal an officer goes through can be tremendous. As one officer relates. "Every time I'm on the stand they [defense lawyers] made me feel guilty as hell." The pressures can be overwhelming. Take the case of one officer, who recently suffered a coronary because of undo job stress. After he recovered, he returned to work, immediately to be faced with a court appearance due to a political manuever of one activist group to discredit him in a case that he had been involved in years before. A case that he had forgotten and which at the time of the proceedings all lawyers involved agreed that the officer had acted appropriately. However, this officer, just out of the hospital, was forced to undergo very strenuous cross examination to justify himself. In the end the court case was thrown out but not before the officer was put through the "wringer." Shortly after this case the officer suffered a second heart attack.

From my point of view, an even more reprehensible negative activity is the third problem within this area, the judge's downgrading of policemen in the courtroom. For instance, it is not uncommon for the judge to tell an officer to apologize to the court for taking up the jury's time or to otherwise lecture or berate him in front of the jury and audience. One officer, even incurred the wrath of a judge because he did not have the required laboratory analysis report with him at the scheduled court appearance and, therefore, the case was thrown out. However, the lead time for laboratory analysis was fifteen days, and the court appearance was scheduled at an earlier time. So, it was clearly impossible for the officer to meet these demands,

But that did not stop the judge from increasing the police officer's job stress.

Lack of consideration for the police by the courts as described above is unsettling to an officer. Further, after experiencing a series of these incidents, it is not atypical for an officer to lose his motivation to do a good job.

Why this should so upset the cop is easy to see. The policeman views himself as a crime fighter and gains satisfaction in the belief that he is protecting the citizen. Thus, in arresting offenders the officer takes pride in doing a good job as a crime fighting professional. When the courts release the offender, it is only natural that the policeman feels his professionalism is being threatened. A lot of time, thought, energy, and skill is often involved in capturing a suspect. This professional effort, as well as the risk to physical well-being, goes unrewarded when the courts then set the captured suspect free or impose a light sentence on him. The officer wonders if his skills are recognized at all when he captures the offender and the court rules that he is not guilty. It is no wonder that Watson and Sterling (1969) in their survey of over 4,500 experienced police officers found that 79 percent of the officers agree that, "there is a big difference between whether a man really is guilty and whether the court says he is." It is within this perspective that comments, such as the following, from police officers make sense: "People have no respect for policemen which is the court's fault because no one gets punished," "Crooked politicians run the courts," and "When you make a good arrest guys are let off on technicalities."

It is from the courts that an officer receives some of his strongest negative inputs as a professional. The resulting frustration and anger the police feel towards judges and lawyers is evident (see Fig. 7). One can easily empathize with the officer who said in frustration, "The last thing courts think about is the policeman." It is difficult for policemen to understand why criminals can be let off so easy, why for example, a young man can beat a sixty-five-year-old woman to death and got off with a ten-month jail sentence. The following is one officer's strong reaction to the above case, "Policemen have feelings—they deal in death and misery, but to a policeman the murder (if I may be so crude) of a sixty-five-year-old woman by beating her is hateful! It's a stressful situation to see a criminal walk the streets, sure, but to see someone like that released by a gullible liberal is abominable!" Or consider the following true case:

> My partner and myself were called to a dismal apartment belonging to an eighty-eight-year-old lady. She had been broken into, that is her apartment was broken into, while she was there, by five, six-foot juveniles, one of whom took her glasses off and held a pillow over her head while the others ransacked her apartment, cursing her all the time for not having more, and finally leaving, but not before they kicked her several times and threatened to be back after social security check time.
>
> With luck my partner and I found two good fingerprints which we lifted and filed, several days later we received a tip and arrested a juvenile, printed him and matched the ones we had saved with his. Miracles still happen, the prints matched! We questioned the juvenile and gained the admission and also the names of the other four juveniles involved. When arrested they all admitted their part in this offense and twelve other ones just like it. We charged them all and sent to juvenile court the proper papers. Three days later we learned from one of the arrested juveniles that he had already had his case heard and was given unconditional probation. We didn't believe him until we called and heard the vicious truth ourselves.
>
> The court referee said with a laugh, "What are you so worried about officer you got a conviction, anyway what happens to them isn't your concern." I nearly hit him. Thirteen, old defenseless victims, with no one but us to go to bat for them and some pompous so and so makes a joke out of it. I went to the head referee, he was out to lunch. I tried for an appointment with the judge, he was too busy. I was advised to not resign warrants because that would create double jeopardy, and would result in a false arrest suit because of the showing of malice. I resigned anyway!
>
> I went back to my district, checked my assignments for the day and read my latest assignment. An eighty-six-year-old female robbery, burglary victim, and this time the five suspects were wearing gloves and ski masks.

As the above case shows, police officers know full well that individuals who are released will go right back to committing their brutal crimes or participating in other unhealthy activities. It is not unusual for a particular beat to be devoid of a certain type of criminal activity, such as purse snatching or mugging of older women as long as certain individuals are in jail. Almost the day

Figure 7. "A Frustrated Cop's Feelings toward Lawyers."
(taken from a Marvel comic strip)

after they are released the activity begins again. In many cases
the police may not have proof who is committing the activity,
but it is common knowledge and the circumstantial evidence is
strong. However, when this individual is finally caught, the
officer feels proud, offers a sigh of relief, but only for a moment.
The offender is released by the courts on a technicality, and the
officer is more frustrated than ever.

In general, once one's anger against the court system has passed,
the reaction becomes one of sadness. But for some police officers
the anger never passes, and the officer long carries with him intense and negative feelings towards the courts. Witness the following comment by a police officer, "I am sick of courts! I wish
there were some other ways to seek justice and punish the guilty!
I wish in child-like fantasy that God would go with one of his
miracles and make them all disappear and then create a new way
to give this poor victimized society relief from the vicious animals
we so decently call criminals." Also, after a time, the officer begins to wonder why bother to arrest a person at all, and frustration and apathy set in. Thus, the policeman finds himself at odds
with the judicial system. He becomes cynical and unfeeling toward the courts and their problems. An extreme instance il-
lustrative of this view comes from reports of police behavior in
Brazil. There, it has been reported (*Time,* April 25, 1969) that
the police have taken to murdering leaders of organized crime

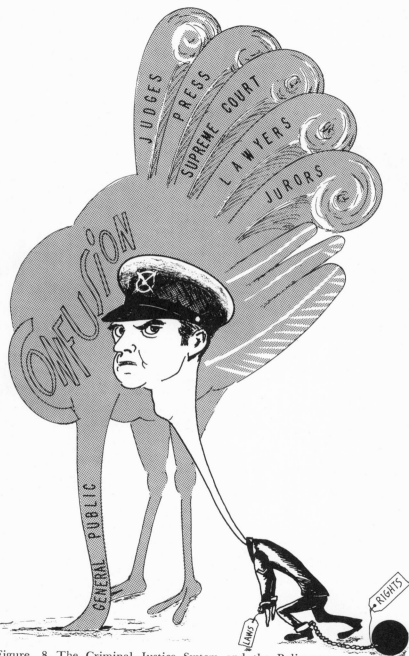

Figure 8. The Criminal Justice System and the Policeman.

out of a belief that the system of justice is itself unjust, and the dangerous criminals would be let off.

Kirkham (1974), in the following passage, discusses the feelings of many policemen in such cases.

> Today's police officer is inexorably pushed toward viewing the entire judicial process as his enemy. He senses that it represents a great and impenetrable barrier which stands between him and his goal of protecting society . . . he simply cannot understand why the preservation of our democracy should require 'crippling' the efficiency of law enforcement.

Adding to Kirkham's comment, that not only is the officer's law enforcement capability being "crippled," but this stressor of courts is so great and has so many ramifications for the officer's well-being, that the officer himself becomes crippled emotionally.

NEGATIVE PUBLIC IMAGE

Unfortunately, the policeman's relationship with the public is poor, he holds a low status job and is disliked by a large segment of our society. But the profound impact of our own attitudes and actions on the men involved in the profession of policing is truly remarkable. This negative attitude on the part of the public finds expression in a multitude of ways. All the expressed ways have one thing in common, they deeply hurt the policeman and leave him emotionally scarred. As Symonds (1970), a psychiatrist and police consultant, who was a New York City policeman for seven years, states:

> The job of being a policeman is unique. It is one of the few occupations in which one is feared, sometimes hated, occasionally reviled or even assaulted in the ordinary performance of one's duties: when we consider that most people need and want to be liked, and that the young patrolman starts his career by seeing himself as an individual who will help and protect others, we can understand what an emotional strain is placed upon him by the uncooperativeness, antagonism and hostility of the public whom he serves.

Almost no other worker must face such negative social action from his fellow man simply because he is a policeman.

The author recalls the poignant tale of one officer whose young son had been coming home from school crying. When the father finally asked his son what the trouble was, the son replied that the kids teased him and said that his father was a pig. The officer asked me, "What can I do? I know my son loves me; how can I tell him the kids don't know what they are saying. It eats me up."

Another officer's hobby was carpentry. His *magnum opus* was the building of his own family home in the suburbs. One morning, just prior to the completion of the house, he found the windows broken and in the living room the word "PIG" had been written in large letters across the wall.

Negative public image is indeed an uncomfortable stressor and as the above incidents show the policeman, must not only endure this stressor at work, but *he must also face it off duty.* Play scientist yourself sometime and notice:

- a place, such as a restaurant, "freezing up" when a uniformed cop comes in for a cup of coffee
- the general uneasiness people feel around a cop
- the cornering and badgering of a cop at a cocktail party over his "reactionary and psychotic" attitude

On the job, the negative public reaction can be as intense. (Note incidents such as picketing, name calling, public demonstrations against the police, throwing of bottles at police cars, etc.) The individual policeman is simply carrying out his duty, doing what his job requires, yet he finds himself in the position of being a front-line representative of the "establishment" and must face the venom of others for something he has no control over.

A recent event may help to bring this problem into some perspective. The relatively modern phenomenon called streaking is quite well-known. At one major college, a group streak was undertaken involving some eighty youths. The campus police feeling uncomfortable and afraid the situation might get out of hand asked the city to send some of their police for support; the request was granted. Upon arrival, the festive mood of the students changed drastically and a confrontation was in the making. The students demanded that the police leave, saying that they have their own campus police, and if there was a problem, their own police would take care of it. The anger, and now ugly mood of the students, was focused on the city officers, *who were only following their chief's orders.* And so, the police were forced into a confrontation in which they had to stand and take jeers and insults.

The following incidents show the variety of problems that can occur under this stressor. One officer saw an elderly lady in what he thought was a stalled car off the highway. When he stopped to offer his services to the woman, she, unexpectedly, berated him and told him to stop bothering her, and to spend his time catching criminals. This is some reinforcement for stopping to aid another human in trouble! Another typical incident concerns the juvenile delinquent who is hostile, disrespectful, and verbally abusive to the officer in front of his own parents. The parents make no attempt to help the policeman and let their son carry on. And what about our own reaction when a policeman stops to give us a ticket? Our reactions often range from anger to frustration with an underlying feeling (shared with the elder lady in the stopped car) of why that cop is not out catching criminals instead of bothering law abiding citizens.

Again try to imagine yourself as a new policeman, proud of your uniform, proud to be a cop, and happy in the knowledge that you have one of the few jobs that really helps and protects your fellow man. Then reality hits. Your uniform instead of representing the positive social ideals you imagined draws forth hatred and disrespect. Confused, you retreat into your home only to find that even without the uniform you still carry the negative label "cop." This stigma follows you around affecting your family and close friends. You are now under real stress.

As any professional, the policeman wants to be respected for his work. Under current conditions, however, the policeman receives negative feedback from a large segment of the population. Instead of being viewed as a hero (or at least as one of the "good guys"), he is viewed as a corrupt, unfeeling enforcer. As a police officer will tell you, he develops a "pariah feeling." His bad public image combined with the public's apathy over, or even active interference with his work strongly disturbs the officer. The officer may develop increased self-doubts or may even come to think of himself as a martyr. The policeman's perception of himself as an oppressed minority has led to the coining of the term, the *Blue Race.*

The policeman, through this stressor, is caught in a most surprising dilemma. Namely, his function is to act as a service agent for the community (with the specific responsibility of protecting community members from harm, loss of property) and yet the same community looks down on him. As Symonds (1972), the police psychiatric consultant states:

> They [the police] consider their function as helping the public, and, therefore, they become upset and confused when they find themselves as part of a group that is feared, disliked, hated or even assaulted in the performance of these services. Some individuals feel that these hostile attitudes are only seen in the ghetto. However, these negative feelings about policemen are openly expressed by individuals from all economic groups. The experience of meeting with indifference to outright hostility of the public towards the policeman eventually results in feelings of isolation and alienation of the police from the general community that they serve. This isolation and alienation reinforces the tendency of the police to close ranks and they then develop all the feelings and some of the responses that minority groups have when they are or feel isolated from the majority.

This stressor is a most difficult one for the police to live with. Some experts maintain that it is the major stressor policemen must undergo. Whether this is indeed the top stress problem of policemen cannot be confirmed as all the research evidence is not in. More likely, this stressor plays the role of exacerbating the other job stressors, for one can withstand problems if others recognize and appreciate the sacrifice. Like the soldier, the policeman will go out there and face the enemy if he feels he is appreciated. But the feedback from the public tells the cop that no one "gives a damn." So with each successive instance of negative feedback his motivation weakens and his confusion mounts. "Why am I despised by the people I am trying to help?" he cries. Something must give, and if the policeman is to continue to work proficiently, it is his personality that changes. And so the hardened and cynical cop develops. But this is a surface phenomenon, deep down the anguish resulting from his poor public image never leaves him.

CONFLICTING VALUES

Policemen are a product of the mainstream of American culture and as such, hold majority culture values. In their jobs however, policemen must deal with subcultures and individuals who have different value systems. This creates the stress of conflicting values. In the previous chapter the stressor organizational territoriality was discussed. In a way, a large part of the stress of conflicting values arises because of the problem of territoriality, but not organizational territoriality. It is the problem of having to deal with people who live in an "alien" environment and who have a distinctly different set of values.

As part of their job, situations arise when policemen have to interact with "undesirable" elements of society, e.g., bums, pimps, prostitutes, drug addicts, etc. And during working hours a police officer is subjected to many circumstances that would sicken the average person. As Joseph Wambaugh put it, "Cops meet an element of society you guys don't see, and they are seriously affected by this overdose of human misery."

Concerning the fact that policemen do see a different element of society, one officer recently related how he had worked in a small town and hated the community. Years later he met another individual from the same community who loved it. The major difference in attitude arose because this other individual interacted daily with the normal society of the town, whereas the policeman did not.

Another police officer stated that when he goes to public places, such as an amusement park with his family, and sees some of the "tough elements," he immediately tightens up in the stomach and his whole day is ruined. Why should this be? Let a policeman explain.

> During his tour of duty an officer has seen an assault on a citizen perpetrated by a youth with certain mannerisms and dress. He then forms a negative feeling against this type of person. The next day the officer is out with his family and sees a group of youths dressed in the same manner walking by. He immediately recalls the previous night's experience. This causes the officer to become apprehensive . . . Since this reaction caused apprehension in the officer's mind it causes a mood that affects his family and detracts from their time together for recreation.

Another type of situation within the area of conflicting values is the stress experience of culture shock. For instance, most males grow up with certain attitudes and expectations regarding females resulting in certain customs, such as opening a door for a woman. In return, certain expectations develop concerning a woman's behavior, e.g. modesty, lack of vulgarity. However, the women a policeman must deal with do not all conform to this social role expectation. As one cop related, he can take almost anything, but he still cannot get used to an abusive and drunk woman. "No matter how many years I've been through this, it bothers me to hear women talk and say things that women are not supposed to say." Culture shock can occur in many settings, e.g. when officers come in contact with child abusers, derelicts, and others who live a most different life style. A middle-class cop may think it horrendous when he investigates a domestic complaint concerning a man who has severely beaten his wife and then be totally baffled when the wife drops the charges and continues to live with her spouse. Culture shock, then, is the reaction one experiences when he meets others whose behavior and action deviates substantially from the norm of what one considers correct. The boy whose parents drummed into his head the outlook that drinking and smoking are bad, that only evil people do those things, gets a severe case of culture shock when he goes to college and finds nice boys drinking and smoking. And the policeman, even though he may come from a more sophisticated background, will see things through his job that will directly affront his mores, with resulting culture shock.

There is one type of situation of a most insiduous nature which falls within this stressor, this is the problem of the bribe or "being on the pad." A young officer, new on the force is often aglow with model moral and ethical values, but the pressure to deviate is both subtle and strong. A lot has been written on this subject and the question of police corruption is a very relevant and real one. As this is a book on job stress little will be said on this unfortunate side of policing, except to emphasize that the pressures to deviate create a stress on the individual policeman that can be quite a torment to him. And if the officer does deviate, the effect of this battle is so great that it has the outcome of changing his entire personality so that being on the take is no longer upsetting to him. Whether the officer succumbs or not, almost all police officers sometime in their career will have to wrestle with this problem on a very personal level (as the recent book and movie *Serpico,* 1973, has shown). During this time of conflict, they are under a most intense stress.

In closing this section, the fact that few can escape being changed by the conditions under which they work should be noted. In the words of one police officer, "A policeman develops a working personality that after awhile becomes so intense that it goes beyond working hours." Thus, the problem of conflicting values goes far beyond the immediate stress effects; it conditions the policeman's personality and his entire world view.

RACIAL SITUATIONS

This stressor is really a special subcategory of the stressor of conflicting values. However, the universality of the problem for policemen and its distinctiveness require that it be given special mention. In general, the problems arising here are brought about by stereotyping which leads the subcultural group to perceive and interact with the police in a certain way and vice versa. The following discussion singles out the racial problem in relation to blacks, but the findings here apply as well to other suppressed minority groups.

Overall, the ghetto citizen feels that the police are not of their community, so the police cannot understand its problems and do not identify with it or its needs. Further, they believe that they cannot receive real justice from the white society, and they became further alienated from the police. In short, preconceived notions, prejudices, and expectations set the stage for potentially stressful interactions between the police and the black. This set would make is difficult for the ideal liberal and understanding black or white to interact, much less the real black and white participants. The point of negative expectation is strikingly presented in Table I. There the results of a survey of 6,000 individuals, black and white, in fifteen cities is given. Note the increased negative feelings of blacks toward the police, even in the older (60-69) age group.

TABLE I
ATTITUDES TOWARD THE POLICE
"Police Use Insulting Language"

Age Group (both sexes)	Believe it has happened	
	White	Black
16-19	24%	55%
20-29	24	45
30-39	14	37
40-49	13	36
50-59	9	26
60-69	8	24

"Police Frisk and Search Without Good Reason"

Age Group (both sexes)	Believe it has happened	
	White	Black
16-19	25%	51%
20-29	15	43
30-39	7	33
40-49	9	32
50-59	7	28
60-69	4	24

"Police Rough People Up Unnecessarily"

Age Group (both sexes)	Believe it has happened	
	White	Black
16-19	25%	49%
20-29	13	43
30-39	7	33
40-49	5	30
50-59	6	26
60-69	3	20

From: A. Campbell and H. Schuman, "Racial Attitudes in Fifteen American Cities," in *Supplemental Studies for the National Advisory Commission on Civil Disorders,* (Washington, D.C., U.S. Government Printing Office, 1968).

The problem of racial situations is a difficult one to discuss because for most, it is an emotional issue. Certainly at times police have been guilty of gross misconduct in interacting with blacks and other minority groups, and there is still racial prejudice in evidence in today's police forces. But much of the problem of police violence to blacks is overplayed or can be traced to causes along the line of individual police officers being provoked beyond their limits. Many police officers work hard in an effort to treat all citizens equally under the law. This is not just a catch phrase but a real working philosophy that policemen follow. However, it is also true that with time the police become quite frustrated and stressed when their actions are not perceived of in this light by the black recipient. As one high-ranking officer told me, "You can't do anything for people, who don't respond with at least a little gratitude." Does this imply that it is the older, experienced officer who is the most prejudiced? Not necessarily, in reality, almost the opposite situation exists. Studies have shown that the more experienced officer has a more mature interaction (is calmer, more understanding etc.) with *all* citizens, and fewer traces of prejudicial, authoritarian responses can be found (at least, no differences along these dimensions are shown) between his interactions with white or black citizens. If anything, the older cop has learned to interact more cautiously with racial minorities.

This problem of conflicting values in relation to race enters as a stressor in much the same way as the stressor of alien territory. The officer must work in what he knows to be a hostile environment. Minority culture citizens do not respect him; they often will not cooperate, and a few even think it a rite of manhood to "off a cop." If a policeman has a strong social conscience, this difficulty of trying to right a wrong and become accepted by the minority community places him under even greater stress. As Ahern (1972) eloquently puts it:

> If the cop who sits in front of his suburban house on a summer evening watering the lawn does not believe all the cliches about "niggers" being on welfare, if he is not certain that communists are responsible for the nation's problems, if he does not have a strong distaste for "hippies," and if at times he does not lash out at every force that threatens what little idealism he has struggled to retain, he has resisted incredible pressures toward evil with virtually no encouragement or support from society.

The problem of the black officer working an inner-city beat deserves special mention. Though they are not working in an alien environment, they are often rejected by the inner city residents for having "sold out to white society." As one black cop bemoaned, "A good number of people view the police officer as someone put in the community to keep an eye on things and the black officer as a traitor, ever willing to do anything to his people that makes the white man happy. It must be much the same feeling American Indians had toward Indians who scouted for the U.S. Army."

Unfortunately, there are also other aspects to this stressor, namely, minority group pressure, minority group interference, and individual racial incidents.

An example of the first type arises when minority group pressures cause a supervisor to ignore an officer's arrest. This occurs because the minority citizen's complaints have strong political implications and are so vociferous, that the command officer on occasion will release the black offender. This, in effect, is a slap in the face to the police officer who worked hard to bring the offender in.

An example of the second type is crowd antagonism during an arrest of black delinquents. Examples of this are numerous, and on occasion have even been given on the spot television coverage. Note the following excerpt from Kirkham's (1974) experience:

> My partner and I were on routine patrol one Saturday evening in a deteriorated area of cheap bars and pool halls when we observed a young black male double-parked in the middle of the street. I pulled alongside and asked him in a civil manner to either park or drive on, whereupon he began loudly cursing us and shouting that we couldn't make him go anywhere. An angry crowd began to gather as we got out of our patrol car and approached the man, who was by this time shouting that we were harassing him and calling to bystanders for assistance . . .
>
> The man continued to curse us and adamantly refused to move his car. As we placed him under arrest and attempted to move him to our cruiser, an unidentified male and female rushed from the crowd, which was steadily enlarging, and sought to free him. In the ensuing struggle, a hysterical female unsnapped and tried to grab my service revolver, and the now-angry mob began to converge on us.
>
> Suddenly, I was no longer an "ivory-tower" scholar watching typical

police "overreaction" to a street incident; I was part of it, fighting to remain alive and uninjured. I remember the sickening sensation of cold terror which filled my insides as I struggled to reach our car radio. I simultaneously put out a distress call and pressed the hidden electric release button on our shotgun rack as my partner sought to maintain his grip on the prisoner and hold the crowd at bay with his revolver.

The following example was originally presented by Jessie Rubin a psychiatrist working with the Miami Police Department. A white policeman on an emergency call to the ghetto found himself having to deliver a baby. Upon leaving the building after a successful delivery he was pelted by the crowd. This incident also points out an aspect of policing discussed earlier, that the cop must be many things (in this case an obstetrician).

The effect of all this is that the stress can become so great that some officers refuse to get involved and will not take action when similar events come up in the future. Others develop a generalized negative attitude towards blacks.

An example of the third type of situation is as follows: a black store owner complains after he has been robbed, because he feels he is not given equal law enforcement treatment. (The treatment he assumes the officer gives "whitie.") This, in a way, is a case of reverse prejudice. The officer is doing his duty to the best of his ability, but the black citizen perceives the policeman as not caring and trying as hard as he does for the white community.

Overall, the problem of interacting with racial subgroups can lead to a great deal of stress due to a misunderstanding of each others' roles (between the police and black citizen) and life styles. The extent of this stress depends on the extent of the communication breakdown and antagonism between the two groups. Generally quite early in a meeting between the two there is a breakdown of communication. The meeting then turns into a confrontation. Sadly, each thinks he is projecting one message and image, but the other, due to cultural differences and a predisposing bias, perceives the message differently. In short, lack of commonality of background reduces insight which leads to the stress of racial situations. Most importantly, this stress arises from a communication breakdown and is *not* due to a lack of compassion or desire to help on the part of the policeman.

LINE OF DUTY/CRISIS SITUATIONS

When one thinks of a policeman one thinks of danger. It is well known that one can get hurt being a cop. Cops are shot at, have their jaws broken and teeth knocked out. And even the cop who has never fired his gun while on duty is likely to have been involved in a fist fight or have been hit by a car. Part of the job of being a cop is getting involved in dangerous situations. But what of the psychological stress involved with these events, the fear or apprehension when one goes out on a dangerous call, or even the expectancy that danger may strike at any moment, or the upset at having to witness human tragedy. All these and more are stressful for the police officer and take their toll on him. These are the stresses of line of duty/crisis situations.

There are two distinct types of problems involved here. One, crisis situations, concerns those duty situations which pose a threat to the officer's physical well-being, i.e. danger to his life and limb. The other concerns situations in which there is no danger to the officer's life, but the emotional situation is potentially overwhelming.

Concerning the former, surprisingly one of the most dangerous duty situations is family crisis intervention, as the odds are quite high that an officer will be hurt. It has been estimated that, "22 percent of police deaths and 40 percent of police injuries sustained nationwide are incurred as a result of calls to intervene in family disputes." Other dangerous situations arise in dealing with drunks, robberies in progress, calls to investigate a man with a knife or gun, high speed chase, etc. It is clear that physical danger is paramount and, initially at least, the psychological component is secondary. The question is what are the long-range psychological effects?

As mentioned in the section on the stressor of inactivity, policemen appear to look forward to crises situations, as these situations are exciting, challenging, provide an opportunity for the officer to use his professional skills, carry with them intrinsic rewards, e.g. the officer feels he is doing something worthwhile and is providing a service to the community and finally provide an escape from boredom. Of course just prior to and during the crisis situation the officer is in an elevated or stressed psychological state as measured by quickened heart rate, increased adrenal flow, etc. This heightened state, for the most part is a short-lived phenomenon, and most of the bodily functions return to normal within a few hours. The more emotional effects also appear to diminish, but at a slower rate. The more tragic and hair-raising the incident, the longer the emotional effects last. If this heightened activity brought about by the *alarm* reaction to crisis situations was to occur on a regular and frequent basis, stress damage would be quite severe, as it is almost impossible for an individual to be constantly *on* and a chemical breakdown in the bodily systems, as well as emotional fatigue, would set in.

Most officers do not get involved in crisis situations on a daily basis. Nevertheless, officers on high-crime beats, for their own safety, must perform in a constant state of heightened alertness. This state of apprehension produces effects similar in the body's reaction pattern to actually being in a crisis situation. Thus, though crises may be relatively infrequent, the cop's body is acting as if they are constant: In this way being in a constant state of peak preparedness tends to wear the officer down as much as if he were in actual danger. In fact, research studies have shown that anticipation before confrontation produces more stress than actual confrontation. For the patrolman, every call has the potential of becoming a line of duty/crisis situation resulting in tightening of the stomach muscles. Fear, uncertainty, anger, nausea, and trembling are common effects reported by police officers in reaction to crises.

Of course the psychological dangers of line-of-duty incidents can be very real and can leave scars on the policeman just as physical confrontations can. Consider the account of the following officer's work:

> I investigated two fatal accidents where three young people were killed in less than one week. I actually had to take their bodies out of the cars and also make the family contact, telling the parents their son was dead. At the time it was very routine, but a short time later when the paper work and investigation was all over, I got to thinking how these young lives were just starting and just that quick it had ended. These young people really thought they were living, having a car, going to parties at the end of a school year, and then, that fast their

lives had ended. I also remember the look on a concerned parent's face. All of this was very depressing. The depression got to a point I could care less about going to work. After thinking it out and talking to other experienced people about it, the depression ended, but the memory of that feeling is still with me.

Here is the reaction of a young officer just two months out of the police academy:

My first radio run that day was to investigate a sick child emergency. Upon arrival at the residence several people met me in the front yard and in a frantic state said that an infant had just stopped breathing. Upon entering the residence and first observing the blue cast skin of the three-month-old infant, I immediately called for the life squad and initiated mouth-to-mouth and nose resuscitation. After arrival of the life squad and their attempt to mechanically resuscitate the infant to no avail, it was my duty to inform the parents that the child was deceased and take their child from them to the morgue and handle all necessary paper work.

To make matters worse (mentally for myself) five months previously I had become the proud father of a baby girl. And for weeks after this incident, besides not being able to eat or sleep, I tried to rationalize why this had to happen and not being able to. I believe my religious belief was the biggest help in helping me pull myself together and face the real world.

And the following reported situation:

One patrolman saw a three-year-old child who had been catapulted through the windshield of a car and decapitated. He went on a three-day drinking binge as a result of the experience, and when he returned he was disciplined. He would not explain why he had been absent for three days because it would have required acknowledging that he had been deeply moved by the experience. And the department didn't know why he had behaved that way . . .

Line of duty situations include incidents in which the officer must face tragic or distasteful duties. Among others, these include situations like telling a mother of her child's death, having to take a dead child to the morgue, being called in on a child abuse case, or having to clean up a body after an accident. In short, the officer is often called upon to witness a great deal of human misery, which is hard on any individual.*

---

*One area of line of duty situations which is frequently overlooked is the stress (fear) that arises when patrolmen feel they are exposed to communicable diseases.

Interestingly, police officers over time eventually learn to deal with most of these distasteful duties, the exception being the helplessness or anguish an officer feels when he comes upon a child tragedy, or the anger he feels when he has to take a battered child to the hospital.

One would think that line of duty or crises situations would be one of the most overwhelming stressors on policemen, but this does not appear to be the case. Policemen learn to adjust to this; they recognize it as an automatic consequence of their job, and though they do not like it they can understand its existence. The police officer is bothered more by the other job stressors, the ones that need not be a necessary consequence of their job. It is these other stressors that break him. The actual real world problems are less stressful than those manufactured by people he is working for or trying to help. Thus, one can say, for example in comparing the stressor of courts with line of duty/crisis situations, that the bang of the gavel puts more stress on the policeman than the bang of the gun.

This is a most significant point. As the stressor of line of duty/crisis situations is one of the few police job stressors that is *truly inherent* to the nature of police work. That is, only the stressor of line of duty/crisis situations is automatically built into policing. All the others are, in part, a product of the way the job is structured and the way the police profession is looked upon and reacted to by the general public. These later factors *can be changed.*

At this point, having covered the stressors on the front-line policman, it is beneficial to take another look at the stress-strain model. A major thesis of this book is that job stress has strain consequences. In this, and the previous chapter, the major stres-

---

This fear arises, for instance, from having to transport ill persons in one's squad car or having to handle drug addicts (who often have hepatitis from use of unclean needles). It is not too uncommon for officers to catch communicable diseases from undertaking such activities. After such events happen to one's fellow officers, the individual patrolman himself begins to worry. Further, his lack of training in health and medicine create an ignorance which allow myths and fantasy to creep in with resulting fear and anxiety in dealing with such people.

sors on policemen have been discussed. Now we can fill in the left-hand side of the stress-strain equation, the stressors block. The completed block is presented in Figure 9.

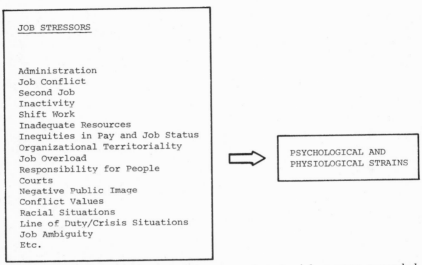

Figure   9. Relationship between job stress and strain: job stressors expanded.

CHAPTER 4 STRESSORS ON COMMAND PERSONNEL

S O FAR WE HAVE LOOKED at the stressors on the front line police officer, the officer in the squad car, on the street, directing traffic. What of the stresses on his superiors, the lieutenant, captain, and police administrator? Does the higher echelon cop have a high-stress job too?

It was not too long into the author's studies of the police before the fact that the police administrators and field supervisors have pressures which are every bit as stressful as those on the field policeman was discovered. As one highly stressed lieutenant told me, "Not once during my ten years on the beat did I take an aspirin, but I went through a whole bottle during my first two weeks as an administrator."

As quite a bit has been said in the two previous chapters on job stressors, in this chapter some of the major stressors faced by command personnel will be only briefly touched upon. But it is necessary to show, at least in a general fashion, some of the ways in which command personnel also encounter stress.

Administration

The administrator's stresses fall into the same two categories as those of the patrolmen: (1) the administrator's reaction to policies and procedures and his lack of participation in their formation, and (2) lack of support of the administrator by even higher echelon personnel. Why both groups (the patrolmen and command officers) face this same stressor can be understood from an analysis of the actual decision-making powers of the administrator. Though the line cop perceives his bosses as being all powerful, in actuality they are also subordinates in the bureaucratic chain with limited powers and controls. The lieutenant has the captain over him; the captain has the colonel; the colonel has the chief; and the chief has the mayor and other controlling city and state officials over him, influencing and dictating policy.

67

So, the command officer (a perceived source of stress for the street cop) is actually in the same boat.

To give some idea of the powerlessness of the command police officer, in the following comment a lieutenant from the New York Police Department evaluates his fictional counterpart, the New York TV cop Kojak. "As a boss, Kojak tends to be a little too critical of his bosses. He questions his superiors more than a boss on our job would. Because we're a semimilitary unit we follow the edict that you obey all orders without question." Another senior-level officer comments:

> The field officer may think of the command officer as having complete control, but nothing could be farther from the truth. The successful policeman, chief to recruit, is responsible for people and things placed under his control. This control is shaped, formed, restricted, and mandated by that which is ordered, directed, or permitted from higher authority.

With regard to administrative procedures and policies, excessive paper work is the most bothersome factor for the administrator. Put bluntly, he is inundated with red tape. He complains of too many forms to fill out, too many cross-checks, and overall far too much *bulk* flow of paper work.

Stress is also created because the administrator (like the patrolman) lacks voice in decisions and policies that directly affect his job. For example, his key subordinates may be detailed out of his command without his prior consultation or even knowledge. This, indeed, is a frustrating situation for the police administrators, as the "powers-that-be" expect them to be good supervisors and commanders, yet they are not consulted in matters directly affecting their jobs. The paradox is apparent to the administrator; he is responsible for law enforcement and, also, the safety and conduct of his subordinates, yet he has little say in who shall be his subordinates, or how long they will be with him.

The administrator also needs to know that he is supported and backed in his actions by his superiors. The administrator wonders if his superiors are not unlike the public, coming to him only with complaints but not providing him with support. Thus, along with the patrolman, the administrator exists in a bureaucracy which is less than supportive and at times even hostile to his needs.

It should not be forgotten that the senior-level officer is a commander, and as such he is responsible for the lives and welfare of the men under him. So he must serve as a stress reducer for the people he supervises. As a result, their problems become his problems, whether they are on-the-job or off-the-job. Therefore, the command officer as an administrator and supervisor not only has his own pressures but must face the problem of his subordinates. When a patrolman gets into trouble, the commander often feels like the conscientious parent worrying, "Where did I go wrong?"

Job Overload

The job overload of a senior-level police officer can be extremely great. Besides trying to perform the duties of a police commander, an already overburdening job, they are required to participate in a host of other and often extraneous community activities, such as speaking or participating in various civic or group functions, attending city council meetings, and other city and public forums, participating in various city, state and federal police activities, and, for the more senior-level officers, getting involved with politics and politicians. Although recognized as worthwhile, full participation with all the groups and organizations dedicated to improving the neighborhood or local community overloads the officers involved. Further increasing overload, citizens with the most routine and mundane problems (dogs barking, traffic citation received, parking complaint, or who just feel like sounding off) insist on talking to the chief or officer-in-charge.

Most of the senior-level cop's overload is quantitative. He has too much to do in a given period of time. For the smaller city police chief, of which there are thousands, this workload may also be qualitative. This arises because the smaller departments cannot afford the luxury of a separate specialist in budgeting, accounting, training, community relations, or personnel. All these activities generally are performed by the chief, or at most by a few of his senior-level men. The small city police chief in most cases is not adequately prepared to handle these diverse functions (typically having come up through the ranks with almost no training or preparation to take over a management function) ; thus, he is qualitatively overloaded. In the words of one suburban department police chief, "In a small department I feel that the command personnel feel all the stressors of the field policemen plus many more. As command officers on a small department, we still have to assist in answering routine calls, direct traffic, and in most cases, work shift work and be on call the same as a field officer." This overwhelmed chief concludes that, "From my own experience I have been under more stress in one year as chief than the previous six years as a beat patrolman."

Courts

The administrator, having worked himself up through the ranks, is all too familiar with this stressor. And the bitterness he felt as a patrolman towards the court system is carried over into his new position. As an administrator, however, his direct inter-actions with the court system are on a more infrequent basis, but the courts still rankle him. The reason behind this is that the problem of the courts strongly affects the men under him, by lowering morale decreasing efficiency. As such, the courts become a direct problem for the administrator. The command officer is further frustrated, as he perceives the judicial system as an ad-versary impeding his crime-prevention efforts. And the empathy he has for his men leads him to "bleed" along with them over court leniency and poor treatment of his fellow officers.

An additional problem for the command-level officer concern-ing courts is that on any one given day 10 to 20 percent of his personnel may be testifying in court. Though many of these officers may be appearing on their day off, either compensatory time or special pay will be involved. This means, in an already stiff manpower shortage situation, the courts are draining off needed manpower and increasing the senior-level officers' paper-work, scheduling problems, and taxing his command abilities to the limit due to his reduced manpower.

Irregular Hours

Except for field supervisors, most command personnel do not work a changing shift routine and consequently do not experience all the problems associated with shift work. However, unlike the average worker, they do not work a forty-hour week. Getting out the paperwork under deadline means that the administrator often works at least fifty hours a week. This added ten or more hours of work a week, too, is not unusual for equivalent administrators in other organizational settings. However, the problem of irregular hours does not stop here for the police administrator. The senior-level officer must always be ready for emergency duty, as he may be required to report to duty at any time to participate in a sudden, unexpected critical situation. Like the old-fashioned doctor he is always on call for an emergency. This plays havoc with the administrator's personal life. Not knowing when he will be called out creates difficulty in planning family, social activities. As with the patrolman, it is almost impossible to maintain a stable family schedule. Overall, the administrators avoid much of the physiological trauma associated with changing shift routines. But, to some degree they too share the psychological effects, due to their working longer hours and being called out at odd hours when off-duty.

Community Relations

This stressor refers to the problems arising from public apathy, negative reaction to, and lack of support of the police. As one captain bemoaned, "People are completely unaware of our mission and are concerned with it only when it affects them directly." A good police administrator knows that in order to accomplish his mission, he needs the public's cooperation. As the police chief of one large American city stated, "A police force standing alone without the active support of an enlightened citizenry cannot effectively control the level of crime in a city."

Crime prevention is a complicated process, which can be made much easier if the public supports their police department. Frustration sets in when the administrator fails to get this support. Frustration increases when the administrator finds himself spending more and more of his day handling citizen complaints and trying to appease the public he is dedicated to serve. The public's lack of appreciation for and knowledge about what it takes to run a complicated police department leads many to unjustly accuse the police administrator of inefficient and biased law enforcement. These accusations often are quite heated, with the press on hand to capitalize on the problems. The administrator is continually on the spot defending not only his own decisions, but also the actions of the men under him.

Off-duty, the command officer faces all the prejudice of the ordinary cop. A cop is still a "pig" in the eyes of some, no matter what his rank. In fact, he may face more adverse pressure, as many people believe the higher command officers are involved in higher levels of corruption and are responsible for many of their city's problems. Further, it is not unusual for the command cop to receive threatening phone calls at home, much to the distress of his wife and family.

Job Conflict

This stressor arises because command personnel (again, like the patrolmen) have to please too many bosses. It may be of interest to note that in a study of the problems of the American worker Kahn, Wolfe, Quinn, Snoek, and Rosenthal (1964) found that:

> Forty-eight percent of the men in the U.S. labor force report that from time to time they are caught in the middle between two sets of people who want different things from them, and 15 percent report being bothered at times by thinking that they will not be able to satisfy the conflicting demands of various people over them.

The police administrator certainly belongs in the 15 percent category. For example, a police chief must contend with the mayor, city council, labor organizations, the public as represented by citizen activist groups, the press and "private" power groups. To balance all these bosses and still get the job done is a Herculean task. Further, senior-level police officers automatically become conscious of the "political arena." As such, they can no longer concentrate (as other senior-level administrators in other industries can) on the product or services their company provides but must contend with the cantankerous political world of their city and walk the tight rope between opposing power factions.

In discussing job conflict, so far, we have talked only of the bosses on top, what of the bosses below? The policemen's benevolent association or equivalent spokesmen, such as a law firm, make demands and exert pressure on the administration, not to mention the pressure that one individual officer can bring to bear. *In toto,* these groups create an enormous work conflict on the senior administrator.

Inadequate Resources

The senior-level cop is charged with successfully carrying out the overall mission of his department or section, namely preventing crime and keeping the peace. Any blockage he meets in carrying out his goal will be a source of stress to him. Frequently he is blocked because of inadequate resources. The administrator often finds that he lacks the appropriate equipment or manpower to successfully carry out his function. Yet he is still expected to succeed in his mission, and failure brings severe pressure on him. Knowing this, the stress of inadequate resources takes on added force for the administrator. The reader may react, "Sure, this is a problem, but it is not an important one." Our research does not confirm this view. In fact, in one study we found that inadequate resources were the second most frequently mentioned bothersome aspect associated with the job of the command-level cop. Take the following comment of one administrator:

> When a commander is assigned an inadequate number of officers to fully achieve the police mission for his unit the failure results in severe internal and external pressure brought to bear on him. This pressure is hard to accept, but at least the commander is aware of the fact that one additional officer will cost the city an additional 20,000 dollars a year in salary, fringe benefits, and equipment. What is really hard to accept are the one time modest requests for equipment, furnishings, or supplies that are required to do the job. I have found it a source of real stress when a commander can not field his officers with adequate

equipment. When two men go into the field with one radio and three other officers are forced into one police vehicle, their combined output is very likely to approximate two individuals, but the commander is charged with the output of five officers . . . How much stress does a commander feel? How much of an affront is it to his sense of professionalism, when he must tell a newly assigned officer that he must live out of the trunk of his vehicle (until a locker becomes available for him), that he must park blocks away from the station because of inadequate parking facilities and that it is necessary to conduct stand-up roll calls because there are not enough chairs to go around.

This same officer goes on to say:

Commanding officers often host leaders in industry, government, academia, and others, and it is embarrassing to conduct business in the sterile atmosphere of most city offices. Besides, when an officer is called on the carpet he ought to have a carpet to stand on, and when he gets reamed by the commander it ought to be while seated in comfort on a padded chair in pleasant surroundings.

Similarly, another police chief remarks:

Inadequate resources can create job overload for all police officers but perhaps more so for the command officer. While policemen in general suffer from the lack of required personnel and equipment, the command officer feels this stress twofold. He suffers from the same inadequacies as do patrol personnel, however, additionally, he shoulders the burden of what can be done to alleviate this problem. Inadequate resources effect the entire department's morale, efficiency, and entire job performance as well.

Job Ambiguity

This is the stress arising from one having to do one's job without being given adequate information and guidelines. Work ambiguity reflects a situation in which work objectives are unclear and there is unclear understanding of what is expected of the worker on his job. According to Kahn and Quinn (1970) ambiguity implies inadequate information which may be inadequate by being incomplete (or in the extreme, nonexistent); subject to more than one interpretation, equivocal; or momentarily clear but rapidly changing. As part of his job, the police administrator, almost daily, is faced with all four of these situations.

A particularly harsh case of job ambiguity arises for the police administrator when he is forced to make decisions based on quite sketchy information. When an emergency arises, it demands decisive action. These decisions may have life and death consequences, the administrator makes the decision knowing full well that he is the one who will be held accountable by both the public and his superiors should his decision prove to be the wrong one.

Work ambiguity is also created for police administrators by the lack of clarity concerning the scope of their function. This relates to the general problem of the role of the police in the community. Are they crime fighters, peace keepers, or social servants? This major conflict over the role of the police leads to a great deal of the ambiguity in the command officer's role.

As with the patrolman, there are other stressors on the senior-level police officer (such as responsibility for people). However, the stressors described in this chapter will suffice to give a feel for the pressures a police administrator experiences. Forced to choose, the author would have to say that the cop on the street has the more stressful job; however, the administrator is running a close second. His job has more powerful job stressors in it than most other occupations in America today.

A thread woven throughout the presentation of stress on line policemen, is that behind each discreet stressor there lies a general effect, resulting from the affront to the officer's sense of professionalism and self-image. For the administrator, too, there is woven through the specific individual stressors an underlying component, the Man-in-the-Middle syndrome.

It seems apparent that a great deal of the administrator's psychological job stress stems from the fact that he is caught in the middle. Besides the pressure from his subordinates he is directly responsible both to the community and to the higher-level police administration for his own actions and the conduct and efficiency of his subordinates. When complaints are made it is the administrator who must directly bear the wrath of the public and higher echelon supervision. No matter how conflicting the demands of the community might be, the administrator must answer to their complaints. When he makes a decision which is subsequently considered wrong, he will be held accountable for its consequences.

Concerning the pressure from below, it is clear that many of the patrol car officers perceive their administrators as responsible for some measure of their job stress and react accordingly. The administrator, however, feels helpless. He, too, is subject to the dictates of higher echelon personnel and the community at large. His helplessness is clearly exmplified in the matter of transfer of officers. The patrol car officer is often angry at his boss for being transferred, yet the administrator is also upset because he may have had no say in the matter. Similarly, the administrator is aware of the need for more well-maintained equipment but is unable to supply it. Indeed, the administrator has complaints about his bosses which are similar to those of the lower-ranking officer. He has little to say in matters that directly affect his job, and he worries about support from his superiors as does the patrolman. The administrator shares an unenviable position with the factory foreman, a cog caught between two warring groups. And like the foreman he bears the scars (ulcers, heart attack, overweight, divorce) to show it.

CHAPTER 5 STRAIN, THE EFFECTS OF STRESS

S O FAR, THE READER is asked to assume that job stress has powerful effects on the individual worker and his family. If this had been a technical treatise, this relationship would have been documented using stress-and-strain consequences, citing liberally from the hundreds of relevant research reports that strongly indicate that highly stressed occupations or workers show significantly higher negative strain consequences. However, since this book is not intended as a scientific treatise, the following chapter will be an attempt at a cursory explanation of the stress-strain relationship citing only those studies the author considers most relevant to the police profession.

Contrary to common belief, extreme job stress does not lead just to mental breakdown, hypertension, or ulcers. An excessive degree of job stress can affect an individual in a variety of ways, or *in toto*. Grouped into broad categories, job stress can affect health, personality, and/or job performance. Within each of these general areas is an almost infinite potential for variation of the nature of behavioral or physiological effect due to individual differences and unique situational characteristics.

To give a feel for the ubiquity of the effect of stress on an individual, one research study, that of Margolis, Kroes and Quinn (1974) will be cited. In this study, a representative national sample of 1,496 employed persons was surveyed, to determine the strength and direction of the relationship between job stress and various strain indicators. As part of the analysis, the workers were divided into three groups, those experiencing low, medium, and high job stress. The results are presented in Table II. Note, that for all ten strain indicators, those experiencing low job stress showed higher job-related motivation and satisfaction and had fewer mental and physical health problems than those experiencing medium job stress. In turn, those experiencing average job stress had fewer problems than those experiencing high job stress. For those statistically inclined, all but one of these relationships is statistically significant at the .001 level. The exception, being the frequency of suggestions to employer (to help understand this category, think of the employee suggestion boxes visibly posted in so many offices and plants) which although not statistically significant also was in the expected direction, that is, those experiencing the lowest level of job stress submitted more suggestions than those experiencing average job stress, who, in turn, submitted more suggestions than those experiencing high job stress. The data shows (as does so much of our research on job stress) the importance of job stress to the health and well-being of the individual. It is a sad commentary that so little attention is paid to the area. In fact, to emphasize this lack of attention, the above-quoted article was entitled, "Job Stress: an Unlisted Occupational Hazard."

TABLE II

RELATIONSHIP OF TEN STRAIN INDICATORS TO OVERALL JOB STRESS
AMONG 1,496 EMPLOYED PERSONS

| Strain Indicator | Overall Job Stress | | |
	Low	Medium	High
Overall Physical Health	+	0	—
Escapist Drinking	—	0	+
Depressed Mood	—	0	++
Self-esteem	+	0	— —
Life Satisfaction	+	0	— —
Job Satisfaction	++	+	— —
Motivation to Work	+	0	— —
Intention to Leave Job	—	0	+
Absenteeism from Work	—	0	+
Frequency of Suggestions to Employer	+	0	—

Note: ++ = above average
      + = somewhat above average
      0 = average
      — = somewhat below average
      — — = below average

It should be remembered that this study presents the results of a sample of workers drawn from a variety of occupations. If this was a study of policemen only, the majority of the workers would be expected to fall in the high stress group and show a variety of strain consequences. Would this actually be the case? To see, we will examine the effects of job stress on the officers' health, personality, job performance, and home life, respectively. Before beginning this analysis, however, the following statement by one police consultant, Judith Grencik, will help establish that a policeman is a whole being, and that whatever the particular strain effect, the policeman's job is going to get to him.

> I think we often forget that policemen are people. For a long time, policemen seem to have been in a category outside of people. Putting on a uniform immediately made them immune from problems of security, the questions they have about themselves, their jobs, and you can send them to do many things and they do it . . . I think as soon as we can discover and again know that a policeman is a man, is a human, then we will know that the job is going to affect him in the same way that our jobs affect us. But the job is probably going to affect him more because of the type of activities that he is called upon to carry out day by day. As social scientists we can usually choose our clientele; if we don't think we can help a person or if they really turn off we say okay, I won't accept you as a client. The policeman doesn't have that liberty. He has to take whomever the radio call says and yet we criticize him when he fails.
>
> So it's quite naive on our part to think that given this type or set of circumstances in the kind of job role that we've given to a policeman, that his job is not expected to have an effect upon him.

HEALTH

The extreme health-strain consequence of job stress is, of course, death. For a moment, let us consider some possible relationships between work stress and three particular causes of death: arteriosclerotic heart disease, suicide, and diabetes mellitus. Coronary heart disease accounts for about one third of all deaths in the United States each year; for working men it is *the* major fatal disease. The evidence linking psychological job stress to coronary heart disease is growing, as is the number of researchers who have concluded that stress is a more important factor in the etiology of coronary heart disease than diet, smoking, and exercise *combined* (for a good nontechnical summary see McQuade, 1972). If these conclusions are valid, one would expect occupations showing unusually high mortality rates with respect to CHD to be highly stressed occupations.

Suicide and its relation to stress is self-evident. If we find higher suicide levels in certain occupations, then it is safe to suggest that the significant stressors are those related to the job.

The relationship between diabetes and stress at first glance appears more obscure, although some medical researchers have found that the onset of diabetes is related to periods of high job stress or emotional upset. Thus it would be expected that high-stress occupations will display higher morbidity rates for this disease. Further, the following radical hypothesis is offered: the mortality (death) rate for diabetes should differ to an even greater extent than the morbidity (diagnosed disease) rate. The reason for this lies in the nature of the disease and curative agents. Once diabetes is diagnosed, proper diet and insulin treatment will usually keep it under control and the person may live a long life. Mortality, then, from this disease (especially for persons under 60) is closely connected (most likely) with the psychological factors which cause individuals to disregard diet or insulin level. In fact, failure to take proper insulin treatment may be a subtle form of suicide.*

With this as background, let us look at some occupational mortality ratios for these three causes of death. The most extensive data on death by disease and occupation was based on 1950 census data (Guralnick, 1963). From Table III it is seen that no occupation exceeds policemen in all three causes, and only one exceeds them on two. When we look at the supposedly high stress learned professions (see Table IV) in comparison to policing, we get a better picture of just how high the rates are.

In considering the 1950 data another relevant and appalling finding is evident. There were almost twice as many deaths (94) by suicide as by homicide (54) for policemen. Policing is considered to be a hazardous occupation since policemen are in danger of being shot at, attacked, or harmed in fights. Yet, in spite of this, more policemen killed themselves than were killed

---

* The importance of diabetes mellitus as a major disease entity is often overlooked. However, in 1974 for example, it was the sixth highest cause of death in the United States.

by others. The fact that only two other occupations evidenced higher suicide rates than policing, and that more policemen die from self-inflicted injury than from injury by others, surely,

TABLE III

STANDARD MORTALITY RATIO FOR SPECIFIC CAUSES OF DEATHS IN SELECTED OCCUPATIONS AMONG MEN 25 TO 59 YEARS OF AGE, 1950 [1]

Occupation[2]	Arteriosclerotic Heart Disease	Diabetes Mellitus	Suicide
Policemen, Sheriffs, and Marshals	202 [3]	200	176
Tailors and Furriers	209	—[4]	—
Taxicab Drivers and Chauffers	244	—	—
Barbers, Beauticians, Manicurists	—	243	—
Cooks, except private household	237	229	—
Elevator Operators	340	—	—
Firemen, Fire Protection	221	—	—
Longshoremen and Stevedores	207	—	—
Lumbermen, Raftsmen, and Woodchoppers	—	—	184
Laborers (Machinery including electrical)	—	—	200
Laborers (transportation equipment)	217	—	—
Laborers (transportation, except railroad)	300	—	—

[1] From Guralnick, L. *Mortality by Occupation and Cause of Death.* U.S. Public Health Service Vital Statistics Special Reports, *53* (3), 1963.

[2] The occupations listed are the only ones out of 149 occupations that exceeded the occupation of policemen in at least one of the above categories.

[3] Figures represent standard mortality ratio, 100 is considered average.

[4] Dashes represent standard mortality ratios below those found among Policemen, Sheriffs, and Marshals for respective disease entities.

TABLE IV

COMPARISON OF 1950 STANDARD MORTALITY RATIOS FOR POLICEMEN, SHERIFFS AND MARSHALS WITH FOUR OTHER PROFESSIONS ON THREE SPECIFIC CAUSES OF DEATH

Occupation	Arteriosclerotic Heart Disease	Diabetes Mellitus	Suicide
Policemen, Sheriffs, and Marshals	202	200	176
Lawyers and Judges	—*	139	76
Physicians and Surgeons	—	125	111
Social Scientists	—	85	—
College Presidents, Professors, and Instructors	—	—	—

* Standard mortality ratios not calculated because of the small number of deaths in the category for that profession.

points out that policing is a high stress occupation. Further enhancing this view is the fact that the figures on suicide for policemen are artificially low, and in actuality policemen probably ranked highest in most deaths by suicide.

By way of explanation of why the suicide rate for police is artificially deflated, the following actual case history is cited. A policeman was found dead in his home from a bullet wound. The barrel of his revolver was found in his mouth with his finger still on the trigger. The official cause of death, however, was listed as accidental. Why the variance of the official finding? Simple, his fellow police officers were the first ones to arrive at the scene of the tragedy. They knew that his widow and children would get a higher insurance benefit if the death were listed as accidental (some insurance companies pay no benefits for death by suicide). So, they altered the facts a little in reporting their finding. This is a typical case. Other officers who have committed suicide actually fixed their death so that it appeared accidental. Again, with the purpose of helping those they left behind.

The data are from the year 1950 (an age before student riots, excessive police-community friction, etc.), what of today? Unfortunately, more recent comprehensive and comparative health statistics are not available. We may read that there is a high suicide rate among policemen in New York and that the leading cause of Bureau of Compensation claims among police officers in the state of California is cardiovascular disorders and ulcers, or that in one major police department over 20 percent of the officers have a serious drinking problem, or in another, approximately 600 officers reported having stress-related problems, but we can only conjecture that policing is still one of the highest stress occupations. But one need only ride around in a squad car with a patrolman to note the patent medications, such as Tums®, readily within the officer's reach to realize that something is going on, or look at the medical histories of policemen to see an overabundance of health problems (too many problems to just write off as a consequence of aging). If that is not enough, psychiatrists have blessed the research literature with case histories of mental health problems of policemen, and newspapers have played up incidents of policemen finally breaking under stress and losing control.

The author believes that police work is even more stressful than it was in the 1950s. This is due to (1) the events that have taken place in America in the past decade, such as the student movement, which can only have had a detrimental effect on the individual policeman, and (2) because of the many cries for help received from police departments or police associations.

Concerning the public attitude toward police, efforts of individuals such as author Joseph Wambaugh notwithstanding, police have come to represent, for a large segment of our society, a very negative image. Public antagonism over the years can only have added to the already overwhelming stress that the policeman must face in his job.

Concerning the calls for help, to give an indication of the extent of the tragedy in human lives and misery, the following excerpt presents a written request by a representative of a medium-size police department.

> Dear Dr. Kroes,
> Information supplied to me by the International Association of Chiefs of Police indicated that you have involved yourself in program directed at stress leading to family problems among police officers.
> Our department is now experiencing problems in this area, specifically divorce and suicide. We are anxious to assist our officers in whatever way we can . . .

(In responding to the above situation the author learned that an overabundence of heart attacks and other stress-related health problems were also in evidence.)

We have been talking of the health effects of police job stress in terms of definite overt health symptoms, e.g. ulcers, and heart attack, but it is well to remember that long before a physical health problem is evident, job stress is causing physiological changes in the body which precede the health breakdown. The pioneering medical researcher in the field of stress, Hans Selye, found that there is a "nonspecific response of the body to any demand made upon it." This nonspecific physiological response appears to be a phylogenetically old adaptive response pattern which originally prepared the human organism for fight or flight.

In short, our caveman ancestors needed every ounce of energy they could to survive in their predatory and hostile world. In response to crossing the path of a saber-tooth tiger our ancestors needed to instantaneously muster all bodily resources, if they were to compete and survive. Thus, built into the human biological system were adaptive physiological reactions that aided in survival. For example, upon sudden awareness of danger, into the blood rushed sugar to provide needed energy. Also to increase the energy level, pulse, and blood pressure were stimulated. Chemical messengers were dispersed to signal the digestive processes to stop (no need to waste needed resources in digesting food when survival was at stake), to signal the spleen to increase the supply of red blood cells to aid the respiration system in taking in oxygen and releasing carbon dioxide, to signal the blood to be ready to coagulate in case of a wound (to reduce the loss of blood), and so on. All this and more took place in a millisecond, so that our ancestors were ready for fight or flight.

In the twentieth century predatory animals (the job stressors of the past) are no longer a major threat, but we still react to the job stressors of today (the stressors for police of negative public image, administration, job conflict, the courts, etc.) physiologically the same way our caveman ancestors did.

Further complicating this problem are the chemicals which turn these physiological adaptive reactions on (pro-inflamatory hormones) and chemicals to turn them off (anti-inflamatory hormones), lest we become overcome by the strong effects of the physiological adaptive reactions themselves (which can be as harmful as the original danger they were called up to defend against). As Selye states, "The process of adaptation may itself become the immediate cause of diseases, namely of derangements due to maladaption. Among these are some of the most common fatal diseases of man, such as the hypertensive, the 'rheumatic' and the 'degenerative' or 'wear-and-tear' disease of old age; the psychosomatic syndromes probably also belong to this group." Thus, this wear and tear on the policeman's system due to these continued physiological changes caused by on-the-job stress can lead to a disruption of this balance and eventually to breakdown and serious health problems. So, these little irritants or job stressors that occur daily in the life of the police officer are having an effect on him "within the skin" that over time can be most harmful.

One caution, as previously stated we do not yet have uniform and definitive data available on the health status of police in the 1970s, therefore, the statement that psychological job stress is the major factor in the etiology of health problems in policemen can be offered only as a hypothesis.

When one considers the health consequences of police job stress one might also look at accidents as having definite health implications. It has been found that policemen have a surprisingly high number of automobile accidents which occur in conditions where no high speed chase is involved and, therefore, there is no reason for increased accident risk. The relationship between life or job stress and accidents has already been established for individuals in various occupations, may this relationship not also hold for policing?

In closing this section, it should be mentioned that with over 450,000 people in the policing profession, there is bound to be great variety in the kinds of health problems individuals will develop. Predisposing individual weaknesses, unique environmental influences, individual stress coping habits, whether an individual seeks timely help or not, all interact with the individual to influence the degree and type of strain consequences he will show. To give an idea of the variety of health problems that can ensue, the following problems are just a few of those that may be caused or exacerbated by psychological job stress: asthma, hay fever, thyroid, repeated skin trouble, arthritis, obesity, hypertension, heart disease, diabetes, ulcers, tuberculosis, migraine, and various mental disorders. Jacobi (1976) gives a somewhat fuller statement of the potential strain consequences of work stress. Psychological stress produces not only what is commonly thought of as being frank mental and emotional disturbance, neurosis and psychosis, personality regressions, brain damage-related problems known as organic brain syndromes, and so-called traumatic neurosis also known as combat neurosis, gross stress reaction, or transient situational disturbances often resulting from life and limb threatening situations or other line-of-duty crises, but also produces a whole gamut of psychophysiological disturbances that, if intense and chronic enough, can lead to demonstrable organic disease of varying severity. A list of such psychophysiological conditions that lead to medical and surgical conditions includes: psychophysiological disorders of the skin such as neurodermatitis and atopic dermatitis; of the musculoskeletal system such as backache (the low back syndrome) , muscle cramps, tension headaches, stiff neck; psychophysiological respiratory disorders such as bronchial asthma, hyperventilation syndrome; psychophysiological cardiovascular disorders such as high blood pressure, tachycardia, arrhythmias, vascular spasms, migraine headaches; psychophysiological gastrointestinal disorders such as peptic ulcer, chronic gastritis ulcerative and mucous colitis, constipation, hyperacidity, pyloric spasm, heartburn, irritable colon, gastroesophageal reflux; psychophysiological genitourinary disorders such as disturbances in urination, sexual functioning, impotency; and psychophysiological endocrine disorders such as diabetes mellitus, thyroid disorders, adrenal disorders, pituitary disorders, menstrual disorders, and other sexual hormone disorders.

Personality

The negative effect of police work on personality is something those of us close to the field take for granted. Unfortunately few have undertaken the task of systematically documenting the exact effects. In the absense of definitive research we must turn to other monitors. A most sensitive monitor of the personality change in police officers is their wives. Get a group of police wives together to talk freely and you will find that they nearly all have noticed a personality change that occurs relatively early in their husbands career. Part of this perceivable change has been labeled the John Wayne Syndrome. As Martin Reiser (1973) , police psychologist with the Los Angeles police department, puts it:

> This is a condition in which the individual tends to swagger and talk tough. He is somewhat badge-heavy in manner, feels that emotion is unhealthy and tends to keep his feelings locked inside under tight control. He feels he must always be right and cannot admit his fallibility or making a mistake. The philosophy is to shoot from the hip and ask questions later.

In some way this is a period when the officer is "feeling his oats." He too is a victim of the television image of the cop and his new authority and awe at his overall mission, keeping the streets clean from crime, goes to his head.

Popular newspaper columnist, Dr. Joyce Brothers recently devoted her attention to the personality changes that occur in new policemen.

HUSBAND CHANGED

Dear Dr. Brothers: My husband joined the police force six months ago, two years after we were married. We knew each other a long time before we finally decided to get married and I thought I knew everything about him, but since he's become a policeman he's changed. I'm afraid I'm falling out of love with him and this worries and depresses me. He seems to have become bitter and angry and this isn't the man I married.

He seems to be much more aggressive toward me and the children by my former marriage. He's quick-tempered and has a negative attitude about everybody. Our friends have noticed this change too and I think they're hurt by his sharp remarks more than he realizes. He seems quick to take offense and he misinterprets perfectly innocent remarks as attacks on him. I'm so upset by these changes that if something doesn't change soon I may consider getting a divorce.—O.B.

Dear O.B.: Before you seriously consider divorce give your marriage a second chance and think about getting outside counselling. Your husband is in a difficult, trying profession and he would probably profit from professional advice that could help to restore and revive your marriage.

Most police officers start out as well-adjusted idealists, but because of the stresses of their work they may undergo personality changes. These changes can occur within as little as three months and may contribute to the negative public image of police.

Studies by Dr. William H. Kroes, a Cincinnati psychologist, showed that police enter their work as eager idealists, wanting recognition, wanting to do what's right, seeking responsibility and hoping to contribute to society. Soon, the stresses of the work give them what he calls a John Wayne Syndrome. They become overserious, cynical, emotionally withdrawn, and authoritarian. He feels the high rate of alcoholism, ulcers, suicide and heart attacks among police are closely related to the severe stresses of their work.

When you consider public hostility toward the police, it's not too surprising that they may consider the world their enemy. I don't know what your husband did before he became a policeman but change of job alone can contribute to stress. Any great change, even a pleasant one, produces stress. People react differently to stress, some become physically ill, some become depressed, and others become hostile and angry.

Many policemen, because of the stress in their jobs, have a desire to associate primarily with other policemen and their families when they are off the job. Often, they even move into different communities just to be with some of their fellow officers. This isn't usually wise because it only increases their feelings of suspicion toward all outsiders.

It will be to your advantage and his if you can help your husband through this difficult period and reassure him that his old friends will continue to be his friends if he's willing to accept them and give them a chance. It will help him in his job if he spends more of his off-duty time with civilians or nonpolice, as this helps to give him some perspective on the outside world.

Try to remember that through most of your husband's work day, he sees only the worst in mankind. If he is a sensitive man, this is bound to affect him. You can save your marriage if you will try to talk with him, to express your feelings honestly, and also to give him understanding.

For most cops this is a relatively short-lived phenomenon, for reality rudely breaks into their dream world. The stresses of their job eventually hit them, and they become aware of the true nature of a policeman. As such, many young police officers go from being idealistic, eager, wanting recognition, and desiring responsibility to being cynical, overserious, emotionally withdrawn, and authoritarian in a relatively short period of time.

With this change the young cop has arrived; he has developed his working personality. Most policemen who have undergone this hardening process show a more rigid, cynical attitude. This came about because of the many stresses of their job: of having to interact on a daily basis with undesirable elements of society, and of being placed in frequent antagonistic/conflict situations. Unfortunately, the general public sees only the resultant attitude and does not appreciate the pressures which lead policemen to develop this protective, hardened attitude.

Along with this hardened attitude another major resultant of the stressors and conflicts in policing is a deadening of affect. This deadening of emotionality is much the same thing that Kornhauser (1965) found in the automotive workers in Detroit. These workers had lost much of their zest for life, had been beaten down, and existed at a level far below their human potential.

Overall, these personality changes follow very closely what Hans Selye has termed the General Adaptation Syndrome (G.A.S.). Selye in his medical studies found that the body's physiological response to stress develops in three stages: an initial alarm reaction, followed by the stage of resistance, and finally the stage of exhaustion. Selye (1973) defines the three stages as follows:

A. Alarm Reaction. The body shows the changes characteristic of the first exposure to a stressor . . . At the same time, its resistance is diminished and, if the stressor is sufficiently strong . . . death may result.

B. Stage of resistance. Resistance ensues if continued exposure to the stressor is compatible with adaptation. The bodily signs characteristic of the alarm reaction have virtually disappeared, and resistance rises above normal.

C. Stage of exhaustion. Following long-continued exposure to the same stressor, to which the body had become adjusted, eventually adaptation energy is exhausted. The signs of the alarm reaction reappear, but now they are irreversible, and the individual dies.

This biological stress syndrome is mirrored very closely by the overall human response, especially the personality, and the biological stages that Hans Selye found can be seen in the overall personality changes of a policeman. When a policeman first faces the severe stresses of his job, he is thrown into the alarm reaction stage. He develops the John Wayne Syndrome; he overreacts. Basically he is thrown into a tail spin, and he must do something quickly or go under.

For some young police officers the pressure is too much, and they quit their jobs or show such strong aberrant reactions that the police department is forced to dismiss them. Less extreme but much more frequently the officers show difficulty in relations with others, especially with their wives. Unable to open up to his wife and overwhelmed by what is taking place on the job, the officer enters a troubled period in his marital relationship. It is small wonder that, as has been observed in several departments, as many as 80 percent of the married officers get divorced within their first three years on the job. There are other signs of the alarm reaction, such as the development of various psychosomatic symptoms, health difficulties, and edginess.

To survive this overpowering situation the officer adapts by developing a working personality. As discussed, the officer becomes hardened, more cynical, and rigid. Also, as a group, the officers become more closed in among themselves and turn to each other for group support and solidarity, and so lose even greater touch with the outside world. At this point the officers are clearly into the stage of resistance.

But what is the price for maintaining this working personality? The definition Seyle gives for the stage of resistance includes the statement, "resistance rises above normal." Behaviorally, for policemen, this can be interpreted to mean that to maintain the resistance, e.g. to maintain his working personality, the police officer must develop certain defense mechanisms. And he can only maintain these defenses at some psychological cost to himself.* This cost usually takes the form of the officer becoming more constricted in personality.

Eventually, if the stresses are chronic and great enough, the individual policeman becomes worn out. He can no longer maintain his defenses. So he enters the last stage, that of breakdown, or exhaustion. Here the officer may somatize his problems and develop ulcers, diabetes, heart problems, etc. Or he may develop serious mental problems which eventually can lead to psychosis.

The picture painted here concerning the effects of job stress on a policeman's personality is a fairly dim one. However, it must be made clear that it is accurate. In actuality, few officers escape stage one and two (alarm reaction and resistance). In fact it is amazing that with all the pressures and with so few supportive outlets available that so many policemen are able to avoid the third stage.

Before closing this section, the myth that policing draws the psychotic, disturbed personality should be dispelled. As research

---

*Another stress researcher, J. R. P. French, views the stage of resistance in terms of person-environment fit. He posits that this defensive distortion will always be offset by an *equal amount* of decrease in the two other criteria of mental health, i.e. contact with reality and accessability of the self (French, Rodgers, and Cobb, 1975).

studies have shown, the mental health, personality makeup, and social concern of the police recruit is above average. It is the pressures of the job, the stressors, which cause the young and healthy individual police officer to develop neurotic and maladaptive behavioral patterns. It has been one of this author's major crusades to attempt to reverse this trend in policing. Too much effort, money, and attention has been spent in selection and screening measures for police candidates (in hopes of eliminating the potential psychotic), and too little effort has been expended in considering the organizational and community stressors on police, which turns a good man bad, and means by which these stresses can be eliminated.

Police Job Performance

In the absence of definitive research we can only speculate about how stress affects police performance. Policemen, in unguarded moments, mention that they refuse to leave their patrol car under certain situations. This refusal arises out of the stress that they realize they will be under both during the incident and after, as in making an arrest in an area which may lead to a potentially dangerous racial situation. Here it appears that the officers are not so afraid of the racial situation and the hassles they will face but they are quite concerned about the backing of their administration (i.e. will the administration side with the public and call the officer on the carpet for police brutality, etc.).

In general, some policemen tend not to get involved when they are unsure of their superior's support. Or, as has been found, the need for action to avoid the boredom resulting from inactivity is so great that policemen have been known to engage in marginal activities, such as arresting or baiting drunks or hippies, racing squad cars, etc., just to have something to do.

One could go through the list of stressors on policemen and for each discuss the potential effects on performance. For example, in terms of the stress of holding down a second job or working overtime, one can imagine a performance decrement arising from fatigue. As another example, the officer on late shift work may be sleep deprived or bored and thus sneak a catnap on duty. But no matter what the type of stressor, if the stress load becomes too much for the individual officer, it is bound to affect his performance and strain consequences will start to show. The general effects of prolonged stress include among others a decrease in mental alertness, decrease of physical stamina, and a decreased reaction time. (For some, the prolonged effects of stress can take on a more insidious course and the officer may turn to an excessive use of force to let out his frustrations.) All these factors will interfere, surely, to reduce the policeman's efficiency on the job.

One's job performance, in a way, can be a very sensitive monitor of his overall well-being. If an individual begins to show severe strain signs in other areas, his job performance will also be affected. For example, if the officer succumbs to stress and evidences alcoholism, severe depression, or extreme nervousness, his job performance will be affected. If the officer develops psychosomatic problems, such as ulcers, coronary heart disease, or diabetes, again his job performance will also be affected (if in no other way than that he will have less time on the job due to increased sickness-absenteeism). Thus one can say that almost invariably one of the strain consequences of job stress will always be a decrement in job performance.

There is also one additional hidden effect on performance which results from the officers developing a working personality, e.g. becoming hardened, cynical, and rigid, over time as a result of job stress. As a consequence, his interactions with the public may become less productive and citizens will be less likely to cooperate, and communication breakdown between policeman and citizen will occur more frequently. It is probably these lowered levels of performance, magnified further by the press and the public, which contribute further to the animosity between the public and the police. Stopping this vicious circle through the use of stress reduction techniques and improved police/community relations is vital.

In considering the effects of job stress on the overall productivity of a police department, one may want to look at the ten CPA's (counterproductive labor activities) identified by Herrick (1975). The ten CPA's are as follows:

Absenteeism
Accidents
Tardiness
Turnover
Grievances
Strikes
Inventory Shrinkage
Machine Repair
Quality Below Standard
Production Under Standard

Though these measures were developed for use in relation to private industry (so that one could measure the costs resulting from the dissatisfaction of a work force), one can see the relevance for policing. If these monitors are high, it can be assumed that work stress is up. Also, these CPAs cost, and the expense may be more than a city can afford.

Home Life

The effects of police work on the home are definite and strong. As many an ex-police officer has stated, it was either leave the police department or get a divorce. Some substantiating evidence for the veracity of this statement comes from one study (Police Federation, 1963) which found that of 1,750 men leaving the force, 565 (30%) said they did so for domestic reasons.

In one survey (Kroes, Margolis, and Hurrell, 1974) seventy-nine of eighty-one married police officers felt that police work affected their home life. Specific problems mentioned in order of importance were as follows:

- Being a policeman retards nonpolice friendships
- Being unable to plan social events
- Taking the pressures of the job home
- Wives worrying about the officer's safety
- Negative public image affecting wives and children
- Wives disliking being alone at night
- Police work hardening emotions, so policemen become less sensitive to their families

Further, in that study all but three of the nineteen single police-men interviewed also felt that being an officer negatively affected their personal lives. The most frequently mentioned problems were the loss of nonpolice friends and the difficulty in attending social functions because of the work hours.

In a subsequent study (Kroes, Hurrell, and Margolis, 1974) of command-level police officers in the same police department, the strong effect of the job on home life was again found. Twenty-five of the thirty command-level police officers mentioned that the job had a negative effect on their home life. Interestingly, the six major problems mentioned were the same ones that bothered the line patrolmen.

As a defense against the strong negative pressures on them, policemen tend to close in among themselves, and they turn to each other for support. By so doing, however, they become iso-lated and lose their non-police friends. Unfortunately, the process occurs after working hours and affects the family's social relation-ships with others as well. Basically, as the negative public image of being a cop continues to haunt him off duty, he encourages his wife to see less of people who are unfamiliar with the police profession. Now, his wife, too, must share his burden, and she is put in a dilemma. The pressure on the individual police officer and resulting conflict for his wife is aptly presented by the fol-lowing comment of one embittered policeman.

> The whole civilian world watches the policeman. As a result he tends to limit himself and his family to the company of other police officers to whom his identity is not a stimulus to carping normative criticism . . . The policeman might survive in his own little world but what of his family that must exist in his world and their everyday one? Their usual friends must often be put off when he is with them. Confusion results for the children and often resentment from the wife.

And, the same theme runs through this officer's comment:

> As with all other people who are not masochistic, police officers are inclined to gradually eliminate from their social contacts those persons who create stress in relation to occupational duties. They become reluctant to attempt new social affiliations after numerous failures and a long period of adjustment. Only after the prolonged adjustment period do most police officers begin to actively seek new and diverse social contact with a more mature and more cosmopolitan segment of

society. Many merely retreat to the psychological security of the "police subculture."

The following incident, as related by one policeman (Skolnick, 1967) serves to further illustrate this point.

Several months after I joined the force, my wife and I used to be socially active with a crowd of young people, mostly married, who gave a lot of parties where there was drinking and dancing, and we enjoyed it. I've never forgotten, though, an incident that happened on one Fourth of July party. Everybody had been drinking, there was a lot of talking, people were feeling boisterous, and some kid there—he must have been twenty or twenty-two—threw a firecracker that hit my wife in the leg and burned her. I didn't know exactly what to do—punch the guy in the nose, bawl him out, just forget it. Anyway, I couldn't let it pass, so I walked over to him and told him he ought to be careful. He began to rise up at me, and when he did, somebody yelled, "Better watch out, he's a cop." I saw everybody standing there, and I could feel they were all against me and for the kid, even though he had thrown the firecracker at my wife. I went over to the host and said it was probably better if my wife and I left because a fight would put a damper on the party. Actually, I'd hoped he would ask the kid to leave, since the kid had thrown the firecracker. But he didn't so we left. After that incident, my wife and I stopped going around with that crowd, and decided that if we were going to go to parties where there was to be drinking and boisterousness, we weren't going to be the only police people there.

Some police wives must face the negative community pressure even more directly. Such was the case for one wife who had to quit her job because her fellow co-workers plagued her over an accidental shooting incident her husband was involved in. Another police officer's wife also quit her job because the pressure of too many people calling her during working hours to complain of the unfairness of the police force, the traffic tickets they got, etc.

The effect of homelife on the policeman's job is especially strong for the young police officer. This is due to the fact that aside from the problem of growing isolation because of negative community contact, he may also personally be in the midst of suffering a rude awaking into the true nature of police work.

The stress effect on home life for policemen is unique. Granted, in other occupations one may take his job pressures home with him. But one has to think quite a bit to come up with another profession in which the job has such a profound effect on an individual and his family. What other occupation can you think of in which the wife and children of the worker are vexed simply because he is a member of a particular occupational group? (How would you feel if you realized that your occupation, like the policeman's, serves as a source of ridicule and pain for your children?) Overall, because of his highly taxing job, the officer cannot help but bring his stress home and burden wife and children, who already bear the stigma of having a cop in the house.

In the foregoing discussion the effects of stress were arbitrarily separated into four distinct areas, e.g. effects of job stress on personality, health, home life and job performance. In reality, however, job stress effects an individual *in toto*, disrupting him both psychologically and physiologically. When job stress reaches overwhelming proportions, one can see (and even measure) the profound consequences, e.g. divorce, heart attack, suicide, mentioned in this chapter. To reach this point, however, requires a long incubation period. Further, the strain buildup is continuous. Each time the individual is stressed he has some strain reaction. This reaction may be short-lived, such as a pang of anxiety or short-termed change in the balance of one of the body's chemicals, or may last several days. If the stressors continue, the specific strain reactions build, and then serious consequences result.

How an individual reacts to stress depends largely on his physical and emotional make-up, as well as on other factors which will be examined in the next chapter. At this point, though, we can take a closer look at the stress-strain model (initially presented in Fig. 5 and 9) and fill in the right-hand side of the stress-strain equation, which is done in Figure 10. Note that the strain consequences follow a two-step process. The first step is the initial, immediate, short-term reaction to a specific stressor. Over time the buildup may lead to the second step, a more chronic and dangerous strain state.

JOB
STRESSORS PSYCHOLOGICAL AND PHYSIOLOGICAL STRAIN

State 1
(Short-term
strain reaction
to specific stressor)

State 2
(Chronic strain
reaction, becomes
general state of
individual)

Personality
temporary increases in:
anxiety
tension
irritability
feeling "uptight"
drinking rate
etc.

Personality
psychosis
chronic depression
alienation
alcoholism
general malaise
low self esteem
low self-actualisation
suicide
etc.

Health
temporary increases in:
smoking rate
headaches
heart rate
blood pressure
catacholamine level
cholesterol level
blood lipid level
etc.

Health
chronic disease states, e.g.
ulcers
high-blood pressure
coronary heart disease
asthmatic attacks
diabetes
etc.

Job Performance
job tension
"flying of the handle"
irradic work habit
temporary work decrement
etc.

Job Performance
decreased productivity
increased error rate
job dissatisfaction
accidents
withdrawal
serious error in judgement
slower reaction time
etc.

Home Life
"spats with wife"
periodic withdrawal
anger displaced to wife
 and children
increased extra-marital activity
etc.

Home Life
divorce
poor relations with others
social isolation
loss of friends
etc.

Figure 10. Relationship between job stress and strain: strain effects expanded.

CHAPTER 6 STRESS REDUCTION

I N DEVELOPING THE STRESS-STRAIN MODEL a most important element has been left out of the discussion, i.e. the individual. The importance of the individual in exacerbating or mitigating strain effects cannot be over-emphasized. This central role of the person in the stress-strain relationship can be conceived by the following analogy. Consider stress to be like rays of light, the stressed individual to be like an optic lens, and the strain consequence to be the spread of the light rays appearing on the other side of the lens. This relationship is depicted in Figure 11.

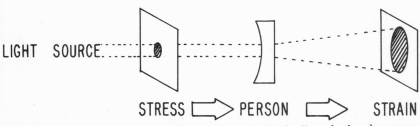

LIGHT SOURCE

STRESS ⟹ PERSON ⟹ STRAIN

Figure 11. The lens model analogy of an individual's role in the stress-strain relationship.

Each individual is unique in his reaction to stress. This is due in part to genetic make-up and in part to individual developmental history, experiences, personality, etc. In terms of the lens model analogy, every human is a uniquely ground lens and will refract stress differently. Thus, even when faced with the exact same stressors, the range of individual responses will vary. This is, of course, common sense. We all know individuals who react violently to a stimulus that minimally affects most of us. This human difference in reaction to stress is again depicted via the lens model in Figure 12.

Though there are a myriad of ways stress reduction may be attempted, they all fall basically within three major categories. The first is to reduce or eliminate the stressor itself *before* it impinges on the individual. To give a ludicrous example for

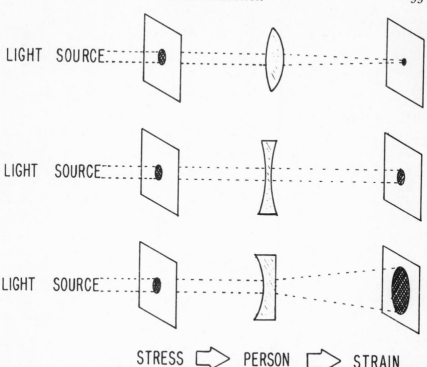

Figure 12. Lens model: Individual differences in reaction to stress.

policing, one could eliminate the stress of shift work for police by having them work the day shift only. The second approach is to change the individual so that he is better able to handle stress. The third approach relies on providing the stressed individual with help from others. This help may come either formally through counseling or informally through social support from others.

These three general approaches may also be viewed in terms of the lens model. In the first approach, the light source (stress) is eliminated or greatly reduced. In the second approach the lens (individual) is reground so that it better reflects (is able to handle) stress. In the third approach, via the introduction of a second lens (help from others) the light rays (strain effect) are reduced in spread. This relationship is depicted in Figure 13.

1. Eliminate the stressor

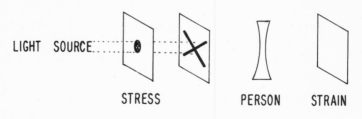

2. Improve the person's ability to handle stress

    a. Initially:

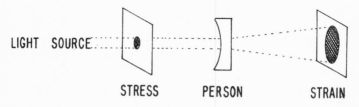

    b. Lens reground:

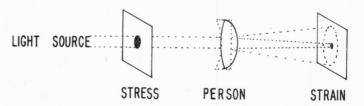

3. Active interaction by others to provide help and support to the stressed person.

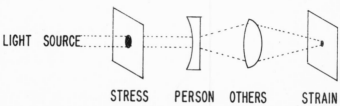

Figure 13. Lens model: Three approaches to stress reduction.

ELIMINATION OF THE STRESSORS

Of the three approaches, elimination is the most effective, simplest to accomplish, and yet, the one most rarely used. The other two approaches generally require either formal training or a one-on-one situation which is time consuming and often expensive as it takes time to train and counsel one policeman. Further, these approaches are inefficient in that only a few officers can be helped at a time. With the first approach, however, the energy expended is toward the stressor itself, so that when it is reduced it affects *all* officers.

If this approach is as efficient and effective as the author maintains, one has the right to ask why police departments rarely use it. The answer unfortunately lies in the nature of the curative procedure; one must deal with the stressor organizationally. The leadership of most organizations, especially those evidencing stress problems which manifest themselves in labor turnover, lower morale, absenteeism, etc. are fearful of opening Pandora's box and looking into the human side of the organization. The leadership is afraid that they will find themselves wanting, that they will be called on the carpet by their superiors. Thus the problems are "swept under the rug" where they fester.

A stress survey was conducted in a metropolitan police organization in which one of the major stresses uncovered for both higher and lower echelon personnel was the administration stressor. Sadly, the problem the line policemen experienced were the same ones faced by higher ranking officers. Further, the problems which the patrolmen blamed on senior-level personnel were in actuality out of the control of these senior-level administrators. A breakdown in communication between the two groups was clearly in evidence. It was, thus, recommended that all levels look at the findings of the study as an aid to opening the communication process and increasing insights. The recommendation was rejected as the senior officers felt uncomfortable and did not want to expose to the line officers the fact that administration was a problem, even though all intuitively knew that this was the case. In short, the administrators were afraid of looking bad, even though in this case they were to be minimally faulted.

A further complication hindering the taking of appropriate action to reduce job stress results from the liberal-conservative dilemma. Just as a college student has an instant negative reaction to a cop, so the cop has an instant negative reaction to a Berkeley graduate, a hippie, or a bleeding-heart liberal. This reaction is carried over by senior police officers to change in general. An intelligent police officer who is interested in improving the situation is labelled a liberal and is thus doomed. This is truly a sad situation. The administration is afraid to "rock the boat" by looking into the human element in policing and the few police officers with good ideas, interested in improving the situation are negatively labelled and shut out of the system. These blocks are a luxury police departments cannot afford as stress has serious consequences and cannot be allowed to continue. Think for a moment how it would feel if cancer was detected at an early stage but those in control refused to act because it was embarrassing, or they did not feel comfortable looking at such a dreaded disease. To make the analogy even more appropriate to policing, how would it be if the doctor failed to report to the patient that he had cancer because he knew saying so would doom his own career?

The problem of stress at work is not a liberal-conservative dilemma and the attack on this problem will not expose senior-level police personnel to difficulties and ridicule. Stress is a problem like any other major human problem. But it cannot be overcome unless it is handled openly and honestly. To the author's knowledge no police department that has actively tried to deal with its own job stress has hurt the senior police officers in any way. If anything, quite the contrary occurs, and the administrator's standing with his men is heightened. The administrator also receives an extra bonus, for as stressors are reduced, his own problems are reduced.

Provided one recognizes the emergency situation created by the immense stressors in policing, how does one go about eliminating these stressors? There are several ways, ranging from hiring expensive outside consultants to doing the job in-house. The latter approach is recommended by the author. No one knows the situation, available resources, and the road blocks ahead as well as those directly involved. The experience available within any one police department is like an untapped oil well; use it.

However, certain guidelines should be followed when working to eliminate stressors:

STEP 1: Determine what the stressors are in your department and establish which are the most significant.

Finding out the major stressors can be accomplished in a variety of ways. The simplest is just to talk it up among yourselves (among all levels of police officers). A more systematic way is via a job-stress questionnaire. (Good police job-stress questionnaires have been developed and are available for use by interested police departments.)

STEP 2: Once the major stressors have been identified, develop ideas, programs, etc. as to how they can be alleviated.

Other police departments have similar difficulties. Find out what they have tried and found successful. Of course, each police department is somewhat unique, but the findings from other departments can be used as a baseline and tailored to fit certain needs. For example, several municipalities have tried to do something about the problem of police and the courts. Some have worked out situations where the officer will only appear in court at scheduled times, times that are not completely inconvenient to him. Other departments have worked out ways to reduce the court delay time for officers scheduled to appear. Or considering the stressor of shift work, one department, to aid the officers in relaxing after the late shift, obtained the cooperation of a bowling alley to stay open all night for the use of its men, while another department has opened its firing range so officers can let off steam after the late shift. One major police department took an even deeper bite into reducing the stress of shift work by changing to a voluntary system in which the officers could choose their preferred shift. Some police chiefs would maintain that this could not be done, that enough volunteers could not be found to fit certain late shift schedules. But it was done; enough officers did choose the late schedule.

Where it seems impossible to eliminate a stress, some have found job rotation helpful, that is rotating personnel on and off high stress assignments to allow them to recuperate and also face as little of that particular stressor as possible.

To foster ideas on how to reduce stressors and to increase the innovativeness and creativity of the group evaluating this problem the following technique (called Green Light/Red Light) may prove helpful. In this approach, even the most fanciful ideas are elucidated and recorded in the first (green light) phase. During this phase anything goes. The goal is to set the stage so ideas flow freely. After enough ideas have been generated the red light phase begins. Here ideas that were initially presented are critically and objectively examined.

Do not overlook the role of selection and placement in reducing stress. There are some areas which may or may not be stressful, depending on the nature of the individual or his experience in dealing with them. If the individual is ill-equipped, he will be placed under stress, whereas a properly trained individual, or one who enjoys that assignment, will not.

There are good potential consultant resources available within the ranks. The cop on the street has built up a wealth of experience and intimately knows the stressors that impinge upon him He is closer to the scene and may have developed some keen insights. Do not lose this highly valuable resource by cutting the line officer out of the discussion process, especially when these discussions concern job stressors that most directly concern him.

This whole area of participation deserves special mention. As previously related, the individual police officer perceives himself to be a trained professional. Further, his job plays a central role in his life.

If the officer is ignored or treated in a cavalier way by his superiors when it comes to decisions that directly affect him, and that he is competent to participate in, his self-esteem will be hurt. Constant affronts to the officers' professionalism can only affect self-image, ego strength, and, most importantly, performance on the job. One way to insure that an officer maintains his sense of professionalism and even grows is to treat him as a professional, rightfully participating in decisions that personally affect him. Do not construe this to imply that the line officers are to take over the decision-making process. But, when an officer is assigned responsibility for a task, or has exceptional knowledge and experience in an area, he should be involved in the decision-making process related to that area. The organization gains because they obtain the use of a resident expert and the individual gains in that his sense of professionalism and stress-coping ability are enhanced.

To emphasize the importance of participation, the work of John R. P. French, one of the leading researchers on stress and the effects of participation, is cited. From his earliest researches (Coch and French, 1948) to his more recent efforts (French and Caplan, 1973), French has found that participation has an important effect on the working individual. In Figure 14 a summary of his findings concerning participation is presented. Quoting from his recent study with Caplan:

> Participation refers to the extent to which the person has influence on decision processes of the organization. To the extent that people's knowledge, opinions, and wishes are excluded from such decision processes, we say that they have low participation. Of course, there is nothing inherently bad about being a nonparticipant. It all depends on the context. For example, you and I are often glad to be excluded from decision-making either because we do not have the time to participate or the need to. We are concerned here, however, with decisions which the person might want to participate in, such as decisions about how he should do his job.

This is the concern senior-level police administrators should have for the men who work under them.

STEP 3: Initiate procedures, programs, and activities aimed at reducing stress in police work.

These activities can range from simple changes in some rule or procedure to the development of a more elaborate program. One caution, if the changes are to be major they should be documented so that one can take a look at the effects and determine if the introduced change was an appropriate one; one worth the costs involved.

For major changes, it is desirable to undertake a true experimental study with appropriate controls, so that one can determine if the accomplished changes are indeed due to the introduction of the experimental variable, or simply because the individuals

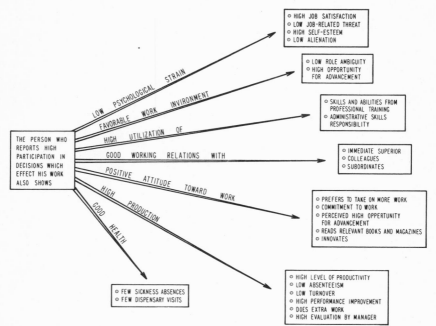

Figure 14. A summary of research findings on the effects of participation.

involved received more attention from management (the Haw-thorne effect).

There is one type of intervention technique that deserves special notice here. This technique has been variously labelled job enrichment, job enlargement, job redesign, humanization or quality of work program, organizational development, socio-technical systems, etc. To the researchers these labels have specific and different meanings. But from the world of work perspective, these differences become unimportant. What is important is that job enrichment does increase the worker's sense of contribution, job satisfaction, feelings of worth, productivity, etc. The phi-losophy behind this approach is that the worker is no longer just a cog in the wheel, an automaton on the assembly line. This approach, in essence, attempts to bring back the pride in the job and reduce worker alienation. The attempt with job enrich-ment programs is to restructure work so that it conforms more closely with human inclinations and needs.

With all this said, what exactly is job enrichment? Job enrichment is the redesign of jobs for the purpose of making them more challenging and meaningful for the worker, along with providing the worker more opportunity for growth, achievement, recognition, creativity, etc. In short, it is felt that by making the work more meaningful to the worker, his sense of reward and his intrinsic motivation on the job is increased.

In terms of actual payoff, it has been found in a variety of job enrichment experiences that following the introduction of these programs absenteeism, accidents and illness, tardiness, and turnover were reduced, and productivity, quality of product, and worker satisfaction increased.*

The police administrator may feel that this is all well and good but it does not apply to policing, the assembly lines, or automobile manufacturing maybe, but not to policing; this is not so. Policing is actually one of the most fertile fields for the introduction of job enrichment. And some departments have actually done so in a minimal way. Witness the new approach of assigning an officer full responsibility for an area. That is, the officer not only acts as patrolman but detective, too. He receives more job satisfaction by being able to take a case through to completion. He is no longer quickly replaced by investigative personnel to return to the hum drum of radio calls. The success of this approach can be seen in the words of one patrolman, who, in speaking of his fellow officers, states, . . . "it gives them a sense of accomplishment, they are doing more than just taking reports after a crime has been reported. They are receiving credit for the arrests instead of someone else. Before they started this policy, many officers were disgruntled, but since then the morale of the men has risen sharply."

STEP 4: A feedback system should be established to monitor the effectiveness of results and to insure that the eliminated stressor does not creep back into policing.

Once initial success has been obtained, there is a tendency to assume all is well and consequently ignore the situation. To

---

*The number of successful job enrichment experiments are fast becoming legion. For a good review, see *Work in America*, 1974 or Paul, Roberts, and Herzberg, 1968.

achieve maximum success, however, one needs to continually monitor and to have an automatic feedback loop built into the system. Work situations are not static but dynamic. Conditions change which may effect the potency of the stressor. Thus, feedback is needed to insure that the problem does not reoccur.

HANDLING STRESS

As previously mentioned, the aim of this approach is to change the individual so that he is better able to cope with the stress of policing. This can be done by giving him the skills he needs to effectively deal with job stress and/or encouraging him to alter his life style to accomodate activities (outlets) that lessen the impact of job stress.

Developing the police officer's skills so that he is better able to cope with the problems of policing in the practical sense means one thing, training. Specifically, there are three types of training a police officer needs if he is to more successfully adapt to the stresses in policing. These are training in stress awareness, insights into self and others, and specific skills training.

Stress Awareness

In order to cope with stress on an individual level, the officer needs to be made aware of the problem he is facing, i.e. the types of job stressors he will encounter and the impact of these stressors on him physically and emotionally. To avoid the shock of the John Wayne Syndrome, the young police officer, in particular, needs to know what policing is really about. Even the experienced officers are often unaware of the nature of the pressures pushing and pulling them apart on the job. They have been under them so long, they just take them for granted. Sure, they remember experiencing discomfort, or remember being mad at this individual or that procedure, but rarely do they stop to think what these stresses are doing to them. It is probably man's nature not to want to known disquieting things. Learning about the stresses in policing is, after all, quite frightening. As one police officer put it, "It's bad enough now being a policeman without having the added knowledge that my health and life are being seriously affected." What this, and most other officers, do not realize is that awareness itself is one of the variables mediating responses to stress. By being aware, the officer is alerted to the dangers facing him, and is better able to activate his protective, defense systems.

For instance, a foot patrolman new to a particular beat is told only that he is to walk down a certain street. The street is well lit and is in an affluent neighborhood. For all intents and purposes, it appears to be a street people enjoy taking an evening stroll along. Now if this is all the officer is told, he too may be in a relaxed stroll-like manner as he walks along the street. But if he is told that in the last few nights a person has been driving down the street throwing bricks at the pedestrians, the officer will take a different attitude. Instinctively his defenses and alertness will be up; he is ready for action. He will be better prepared, and also will be less likely to get hurt. Awareness of the nature of the stresses on one's job can serve the same function. Awareness is a warning, so that the individual may prepare appropriate stress coping defenses.

Insights into Self and Others

Most individuals have an available major, untapped resource to help them cope with stress, themselves. However, this resource will remain untapped as long as the individual is ignorant of how to use his full potential. The officer needs a fuller understanding of his own personal reactions to various stimuli and of what the roles personality, motivation, cognition, emotion, fears, needs, etc. have in affecting human behavior. Why do we do what we do? Why does the other person behave the way he does? What effect does it have when one behaves a certain way to another individual? Since the police officer's job to a large extent is interacting with people he needs to know the answers to these questions. It would be unreasonable to expect a policeman to become a fully trained behavioral scientist, on the other hand there is a body of practical psychology that the officer needs to know and should be trained in.* There are college courses and

---

* As one senior police officer stated, "If we can 'arm' our officers with a basic knowledge of human behavior it can be as great a weapon as a firearm."

instructors around the country readily available to teach these skills. Some have even prepared specific primers directly for police officers.

Not only the individual police officer but police management too needs to become aware of job stress and its consequences, for without management's understanding and backing, programs aimed at stress reduction are doomed to failure. How many potential tragedies are there in a police department now that will go unchecked because no one is aware? One of the most deeply moving comments made to the author in this area was by an officer, who, subsequent to hearing a talk given on job stress stated that he knew of four officers who, he believed, would be alive today if we had gotten out the message ten years sooner. These officers had committed suicide.

To emphasize this point note the following.

Job Stress in Policing

Nothing in police officers' backgrounds or education prepares them for the stress of police work. Nothing in the organization's management of patrol officers equips them to cope with it. Characteristically, the patrol officer wants to fight crime. He joins the police department believing that he will do so. But he finds himself spending 80 percent of his time doing thing which seem to be unrelated to crime. He is told to follow rules and obey orders; but the rules cover few of the situations he encounters, and rarely is a supervisor there to give the orders. He believed that the job would be exciting and rewarding; but for every moment of excitement, there are long periods of boredom; and the rewards are very few.

And no one has equipped him in any respect for the stress of the job. Police officers are not supposed to feel stress. In the first place, they are the law enforcers; and people who enforce the law should be utterly unemotional and impartial, beyond human feelings. Second, the job calls for toughness; police officers must see and do things which affect weaker people. To admit that an experience has been emotional is to admit weakness.

The organization encourages these attitudes. Police officers who have problems are ignored, until their problems are too serious to be hidden. Then the drinking patrolman or the emotionally troubled one is deprived of his gun, put in a corner of the department where he won't be noticed, and confined there often for the rest of his career. One police officer told a story of a patrolman who was found by his sergeant sitting on a curb, twirling his revolver. The sergeant, not recognizing the behavior as a symptom, ordered him to get back into his car and continue patrol. Later that evening, the patrolman shot himself in the head.

Police departments are filled with such tales. In San Francisco late last year, an off-duty police officer, drinking heavily in a bar, got into an argument and killed another patron. Newspaper criticism was violent when it was learned that the officer had been well known as an alcoholic for years (Unpublished proposal, International Conference of Police Associations).

Specific Skills Training

Specific skills training differs from the two previously-mentioned approaches to handling stress, in that, here the officer is taught how to act and deal with *specific* stressful job situations.

A classic example of this type of training is family crisis intervention. As brought out earlier, one of the most stressful and physically dangerous calls for a cop is family fight in progress. How does the officer diffuse the situation; what should he do? Exactly how should he act? We have answers to these questions, and some excellent crisis intervention programs have been developed (the programs of Jeffery Schwartz on the West Coast and Morton Bard on the East Coast deserve special notice). But this information has to filter down to the line officer in the form of actual training. As an aside, the effects of such training can be quite startling in terms of impact on police performance (see Zacker and Bard, 1973).

There are other high probability events besides family crisis situations which a cop is likely to face. Such situations as the racial conflict, the irrate citizen, the cop-baiting students, and the child tragedy occur with some frequency. The police officer's skills in handling these situations can be improved and his anxiety and overall stress level decreased in these situations if he attains the appropriate prior experience. One way to get this experience is through a type of training known as role playing. Via this technique, modified real-life situations are presented in the class, and the officer becomes one of the participants in the drama. Through this experience, the officer learns how to cope and handle what otherwise would have been a difficult situation for him. He gets a chance to make his errors and learn about his own emotions in the safety of the classroom.

Another distinct type of specific skill training is the learning of psychological processes pertinent to police work, such as human communication, group dynamics, personality theory, or organizational behavior. One way to better handle administrative stress, for example, is to know more about the human side of organizations. To do this specific training in group dynamics or organizational psychology would prove useful as it would give the administrator new awareness into the nature and dynamics involved in organizations. Another type of training would be towards developing improved communications skill. Much of the friction in policing is due to either police-citizen interaction or police-police administration interaction. One technique that gives the officer the skills to deal with these problems in communication is transactional analysis, a skill which can readily be taught in the training class.

Overall specific-skills training has two benefits. First, it prepares the individual so that he is better able to cope with specific, major stressors on the job. Second, it helps diminish the potentiality of certain situations even becoming stress provoking, e.g. if the officer is better prepared, what once he considered to be a stressful event will no longer be so. This is because the officer better knows how to handle the situation. Thus he feels more confident and less anxious in it.

Besides training in developing specific skills so that an officer is better able to cope with on-the-job problems of policing, there is another approach to help the individual cop maintain his stamina in the face of chronic job stress. This approach is the utilization of various outlets to reduce one's overall level of stress. The pressures of his job have created a great deal of tension within the cop. This tension needs to be released. One important way for this to occur is for the individual to learn ways of utilizing *tension releasers*. This learning, in effect, is another form of needed training for the police officer.

A tension releaser can take many forms, the exact nature depending on the personality, life style, and interests of the individual. The important thing is that workers in high stress occupations, even more than the average worker, need outlets to channel their pent up tensions and emotions. Even aside from needing to release their tension they need these outlets to help them to relax and slow down, to return again to a normal state of equilibrium. These outlets are useful to help a person recharge his "life battery."

Some of the more generally available outlets are (1) hobbies, such as skiing, boating, furniture refinishing, stamp collecting, carpentry, hobbycraft, fishing, and a thousand more, (2) physical exercise,* either on a regular routine at the gym or activities, such as tennis, golf, or even jogging, (3) taking a vacation when the stress on the job is getting to be too much, and (4) direct relaxation training techniques. These latter techniques not only help a person to unwind but also increase his awareness of when he is getting too tense.

One of the more promising of the relaxation techniques is bio-feedback. As the name implies the individual is given feedback of his biological status. Typically, the individual is hooked up to some sort of monitoring device which registers change in one of his bodily systems, such as galvonic skin response, muscle tension, heart rate, brain wave pattern, etc. As the officer observes a particular body monitor, he learns to change the level of that monitor. As he lowers the particular body monitor, he is also lowering his overall state of tension. Utilizing bio-feedback, a stressed officer can be taught to control an irregular heartbeat by force of his own mind as he watches the pulsations of his heart on an electronic monitor. Another can be taught to suppress an agonizing migraine headache by regulating the flow of blood in his head

---

*Physical activity deserves special mention as a stress reducer. Not only does it serve as a tension releaser, but exercise builds up a collateral blood network, which can be of immense value if there should be a blood clot (for an alternate pathway for the supply of blood is then available). Exercise also has another function; vigorous exercise serves to increase fibrinolytic activity, increase the efficiency of cardiac action, increase cardiac output, slow the heart and regularize rhythm, as well as dissolve minute amounts of plaque buildup.

One caution, there is a distinction between effective physical exercise and intensely competitive sports. In the latter case, the psychological strain and drive surrounding the will to win can be quite detrimental, negating the otherwise positive benefits of the physical activity involved.

and hands. Still another can be taught to alleviate tension and insomnia by learning how to relax the muscles of the forehead. With practice one can become quite adept at quickly reducing his tension level. The commensurate feeling of calm and relaxation is well worth the initial training effort. The importance and revolution of bio-feedback is nicely caught in the following quote by McQuade, 1973.

> Behind bio-feedback is something of a revolution in medical theory. Man's skeletal muscles have obviously always been at the command of his brain. He can will his arms to move up and down, his eyelids to blink fast or slow. But it had not been postulated until recently that man can control his autonomic nervous system, that unseen regulator of interior processes such as pulse, glandular secretion, and oxygen consumption—the chemistry by which the stress diseases are so frequently triggered.

Another relaxation technique of some benefit to policing is neuromuscular relaxation. Here, also, the officer is trained in how to relax his body but in this case by a conscious effort to detect and subsequently control residual tension in muscles (without the aid of an electronic monitoring device). There are other more exotic but no less effective relaxation techniques, such as yoga, transendental meditation and the like. All have one thing in common, they help the individual become more aware of himself and his body and help him to physically relax.

SUPPORTIVE HELP FROM OTHERS

This important form of help can occur in two ways, by aid being given either on a formal or informal basis. Formal help involves professional counseling or therapy. Informal help arises out of positive interactions with one's boss, workmates, family, and friends.

Formal Support

Either an acute situational crisis or a slow buildup of job-related strain to a chronic and dangerous level can cause a police officer to need professional help. In most communities there are mental health professionals available and in some there is an active viable community mental health center. Unfortunately, for the stressed policeman most trained professionals are ill-prepared to deal with police personnel, and though they may be of some help to the troubled officer they are handicapped by their lack of familiarity with the nature of police work, the pressures the officer experiences, and their own biases. Further, the officer is often reluctant to take advantage of these services. There is a general feeling in our culture that to seek a mental health professional is a sign of weakness; all too often a policeman shares this belief. This creates a most interesting situation. Two cops may be under the same extreme job stress, but one develops heart trouble and the other some behavioral difficulty. The former is willing to seek medical attention for his problem but the latter is not, that is until his problem finally becomes a physical one. Then our second individual seeks the medic but still only for the now evident physical symptom and not the cause.

The reluctance to seek professional aid and yet the need to seek help is aptly portrayed in the following comment (Portland Traumatic Incident Program).

> All officers were in agreement that those who had been required to shoot someone felt strangely isolated from the rest of the Police Bureau. Fellow officers, in an attempt to ease the situation, would call such an officer "Killer" in a misguided attempt at humor. It was felt that the need to talk to someone a day or two after the incident was acute. Officers at our session rejected seeing a psychiatrist or a clinical psychologist at this stage, stating that they preferred to share their feelings with another officer who had experienced the similar situation. The feeling is summed up in the expression "Nobody else knows what it's really like."

Because of the lack of qualified professionals knowledgeable about police and the unwillingness of most police officers to seek counseling, it is advisable to have a full-time mental health worker on the police force. This setup has several advantages. For one, the consultant can become familiar with the workings of the police force and the problems involved. For another, the men learn to trust him. The full-time health consultant also is more able to provide viable input to the department in matters that greatly effect the stress on police personnel. It is my belief that money spent in this way (hiring of health consultants) comes back four-fold in reduced absenteeism, turnover, sickness, and increased well-being and productivity. If the department cannot afford a full-time consultant, it should at least have a part-time consultant.

Many books have been written on the counseling and therapy process, and it is not necessary to expand on them. In fact, to do so would take this book in a direction far afield from what was originally intended. Formalized therapy belongs in the realm of the specialist; it is enough for the police department to know that this service is available, and that, by in large, it is quite successful. There is one point, however, that the police administrator needs to be aware of. To be maximally successful, the therapist must be able to insure complete privacy and confidentiality to his client, the officer. The individual policeman must be able to feel free and safe in taking advantage of counseling services. Thus, the police department must not interfere with the client-therapist relationship.

It should also be realized that a good therapist can do more than just provide individual client-therapy. He can provide beneficial training to police personnel in human awareness, group desensitization, specific human skills training, psychological evaluations of potential new officers, and the like.

Informal Support

Man does not live alone. He is part of a larger human society. He is a member of a family, is close to a particular work group, belongs to a certain church, etc. Man is, indeed, a social animal and in time of need social support from others can provide an effective bulwark against the waves of stress. The anchorage in, and identification with, one or a series of groups, e.g. family, work, church, social club, provides the individual with needed support.

Research to date indicates that social support is one of the more important avenues available for reducing job stress. Alone the work stress may be too much for the officer. But with social support from others he is better able to cope. The three major sources of social support available to the officer are support from his peers, family, and supervisor.

At work, his mates are there to help share the pressure, to commiserate with and bolster each other's spirits, and even off-duty, officers typically have a favorite bar or tavern where they congregate. There, while relaxing, they like to hear each other's war stories, and everyone has a story to tell. The value of these war stories goes beyond just the relaxing effect of listening to an enjoyable tale. As one officer in an insightful moment stated, "I imagine with hearing other exciting situations and how other people dealt with their situation makes you feel you can cope with yours."

The following statement by Robert J. di Grazia, Commissioner of the Boston Police Department emphasizes the important role an officer's peers can play in helping him to cope with the stressors of his work.

> Police work has always been a demanding profession, but in the last few years, as it has become more and more complicated, the stresses of the job have increased to the point that they are often difficult for individual police officers to deal with alone. The toll these pressures take on the health and well-being of police officers varies in kind and degree with the individual case, but virtually every officer, sometime during his career, feels their effects. *The success he has in dealing with his particular problem usually depends on how much support he gets from his fellow officers.*
>
> There are a number of reasons why this is so, but the main reason is simply that police officers don't often talk about police work to outsiders. We hesitate to talk to our civilian friends because they don't generally understand what the problems really are. We avoid discussing police work with our wives or families because we don't want them involved in that part of our lives; and we reject "professional" help, either because we have no confidence in it or because it seems too demeaning for a policeman to admit that he's human and needs help. *That leaves other police officers as the only people from whom we are prone to accept advice or assistance.*

The role one's boss can play in reducing job stress should be obvious. A good supervisor can be a tremendous resource and support to his men in times of trouble.

At home, social support from the family helps the tired officer relax and take his mind off work. With family support being so important it is small wonder that time and time again researchers find that the factor correlating highest with police performance is the stability of the officer's home life. Being such an important variable, it is too critical to be left to chance alone. Police departments should make an active effort to foster family social support. This does not mean interfering in the private life of the officer, but it does mean helping him to realize the importance of this resource. There are several ways police departments can encourage and improve family social support. One is simply to encourage a get together between experienced police officer wives and wives of new recruits. The senior wives can relate their experiences and in so doing, begin to prepare the younger wives for what they can expect, the difficult periods and changes their husbands may go through. Some police departments have established more formal programs, such as seminars for the wives on the problems they will face. A few even have initiated joint husband and wife counseling programs. Whatever the approach, this is a most important area; it should not be overlooked.

Concerning husband-wife interaction, the following bears consideration. Many police officers make an active effort to leave their job at work, and so when they come home tell their wives little, if anything, of the unsettling events of the day. This is good, if the police officer truly does leave his job at work. However, too many officers fail to realize that they are, in fact, bringing their jobs home with them. One need not just talk about his work to be bringing it home with him. There are other ways to communicate. The officer who comes home irritable or anxious, who jumps at his kids, who argues with his wife is, in effect, bringing his job home with him. The officer who closes himself off from his family is also bringing the job home with him. The wife wonders why; what can she do? She becomes confused and begins to question the marriage. She wants to help but does not know how. The husband, in turn, fails to get the social support he needs and the situation worsens.

One must learn to open up his emotions to his spouse. A wife is not a fragile, helpless creature; many wives inwardly feel useless and are glad when their husband communicates openly with them. This sharing will bring two people closer and help develop a stable relationship which can then provide social support to the partner most in need of it at a particular time.

As this book is brought to a close, the author hopes the reader has gained some understanding of the importance of the stress in policing and its harmful effects on the police officer and his family. If the reader is part of the nonpolice community it is hoped that he has come to appreciate his role in the fostering of some of the major stressors on policemen. If the reader is a police officer, the words of August Vollmer, retired Chief of Police, Berkeley, California, should be heeded, "The ideal police officer could possess to his advantage the following: the wisdom of Solomon, the courage of David, the strength of Samson, the patience of Job, the leadership of Moses, the kindness of the Good Samaritan, the strategy of Alexander, the faith of Daniel, the diplomacy of Lincoln, the tolerance of the Carpenter of Nazareth, and finally, an intimate knowledge of every branch of the natural, biological and social sciences. And if he had all this, the public might accept him as a good policeman." Good luck, you are needed if not always appreciated.

REFERENCES

Ahern, J.: *Police in Trouble.* New York, Hawthorne, 1972.

Alex, N.: *Black in Blue.* New York, Appleton, 1969.

Ardrey R.: *Territorial Imperative.* New York, Dell, 1968.

Bard, M.: *Training Police as Specialists in Family Crisis Intervention.* Washington, D.C., U.S. Government Printing Office, 1970.

Bard, M., and Berkowitz, B.: The community as laboratory: exploring psychoanalytic concepts. In D. Milman and G. Goldman (Eds.) : *Psychoanalytic Contributions to Community Psychology.* Springfield, Thomas, 1971.

Clarren, S., and Schwartz, A.: An evaluation of Cincinnati's team policing program. Paper presented at American Psychological Association Convention, New Orleans, 1974.

Coch, L., and French, J.: Overcoming resistance to change. *Human Relations, 1*:512-532, 1948.

Cruse, D., and Rubin, J.: Police behavior (part I). *Journal of Psychiatry and Law 1* (2) :167-222, 1973.

Cobb, S., and Rose, R.: Hypertension, peptic ulcer, and diabetes in air traffic controllers. *JAMA, 224* (4) :489-491, 1973.

Daley, R.: *Target Blue.* New York, Delacorte Dell, 1971.

Eisenberg, T.: Sources of psychological stress. Paper presented at NIOSH Police Stress Symposium, Cincinnati, 1975.

Fenster, C., and Locke, B.: Neuroticism among policemen: an examination of police personality. *J Appl Psychol, 57* (3) :358-359, 1973.

Fink, J., and Sealy, L.: *The Community and the Police—Conflict or Cooperation?* New York, Wiley, 1974.

French, J., and Caplan, R.: Organizational stress and individual strain. In A. Marrow (Ed.) : *The Failure of Success.* New York, AMACOM, 1973.

French, J., Rodgers, W. and Cobb, S.: A model of person-environment fit. In L. Levi (Ed.) : *Society, Stress and Disease: Working Life.* London, Oxford U Pr, 1975.

Froberg, J., and Akerstedt, T.: Night and shift work effects on health and well-being. In L. Levi (Ed.) : *Society, Stress and Disease: Working Life.* London, Oxford U Pr, 1975.

Gardiner, J.: Ticket-fixing in Massachusetts. In A. Heidenheimer (Ed.) : *Political Corruption.* New York, HR&W, 1970.

Gardner, M.: Neuromuscular relaxation as a methodological approach to stress conditioning. *Police,* March-April: 73-73, 1971.

Garmire, B.: The police role in an urban society. In R. Steadman (Ed.) : *The Police and the Community.* Baltimore, Johns Hopkins University Press, 1972.

Guralnick, L.: Mortality by occupation and cause of death. U.S. Public Health Service: *Vital Statistics Special Reports, 53* (3) , 1963.

Herrick, N. *The Quality of Work and Its Outcomes.* Columbus, Academy for Contemporary Problems, 1975.

Hinkle, L., and Wolf, S.: A summary of experimental evidence relating life stress to diabetes mellitus. *Journal of Mount Sinai Hospital, 19*:537-570, 1952.

Hodge, R., Paul, M., and Rossi P.: Occupational prestige in the United States, 1925-63. *Am J. Sociol, 70*:290-292, 1964.

House, J.: The effects of occupational stress on physical health. In J. O'Toole (Ed.) : *Work and the Quality of Life.* Cambridge, MIT Pr, 1974.

Igleberger, R.: Police/yesterday and today. *Public Management,* July:20-22, 1974.

Jacobi, J.: Reducing police stress—a psychiatrist's point of view. Paper presented at NIOSH Police Stress Symposium, Cincinnati, 1975.

Kahn, R., and Quinn, R.: Role stress: a framework for analysis. In A. McLean (Ed.) : *Occupational Mental Health.* New York, Rand, 1970.

Kahn, R., Wolfe, D., Quinn, R., Snoek, J., and Rosenthal, P.: *Organizational Stress: Studies of Role Conflict and Ambiguity.* New York, Wiley, 1964.

Kirkham, G.: From professor to patrolman: a fresh perspective on the police. *Journal of Police Science and Administration, 2* (2) :127-137, 1974.

Kornhauser, A.: *Mental Health of the Industrial Worker: A Detroit Study.* New York, Wiley, 1965.

Kroes, W.: Psychological job stress and worker health: a programmatic effort. In L. Levi (Ed.) : *Society, Stress and Disease: Working Life.* London, Oxford Pr, 1975.

Kroes, W. & Hurrell, J. (Eds.): *Job Stress and The Police Officers: Identifying Stress Reduction Techniques,* Cincinnati, NIOSH, 1976.

Kroes, W., Hurrell, J., and Margolis, B.: Job stress in police administrators. *Journal of Police Science and Administration, 2* (4) :381-387, 1974.

Kroes, W., Margolis, B., and Hurrell, J.: Job stress in policemen. *Journal of Police Science and Administration, 2* (2) :145-155, 1974.

Lefkowitz, J.: Job attitudes of police. Final Report on Grant # NI 70-065-PG-12, National Institute of Law Enforcement and Criminal Justice, Law Enforcement Assistance Administration.

Levin, E.: Telly Savalas' technical advisor. *TV Guide, 1118*:20-24, 1974.

Liebman, D., and Schwartz, J.: Police programs in domestic crisis intervention: a review. In H. Snibbe, and J. Snibbe (Eds.) : *The Urban Policeman in Transition.* Springfield, Thomas, 1972.

Maas, P.: *Serpico.* New York, Viking, 1973.

Margolis, B., and Kroes, W.: Occupational stress and strain. In A. McLean (Ed.) : *Occupational Stress.* Springfield, Thomas, 1974.

Margolis, B., Kroes, W., & Quinn, R.: Job Stress: an unlisted occupational hazard. *Journal of Occupational Medicine, 16*(10):659-661, 1974.

McQuade, W.: What stress can do to you. *Fortune, 85* (1) :102-107, 1972.

McQuade, W.: Doing something about stress. *Fortune, 87* (5) :250-261, 1973.

Nam, C., and Powers, M.: Changes in the relative status level of workers in the United States, 1950-1960. *Social Forces, 47*:167-170, 1968.

National Advisory Commission on Criminal Justice Standards and Goals: *Police.* Washington, D.C., Government Printing Office, 1973.

Niederhoffer, A.: *Behind the Shield.* Garden City, Doubleday, 1967.

Paul, W., Roberts, K., and Herzberg, F.: Job enrichment pays off. *Harvard Business Review, 47* (2) :61-78, 1969.

Police Federation: *Police Federation Newsletter, 4* (5) , 1963.

President's Commission on Law Enforcement and Administration of Justice: *The Police.* Washington, D.C., U.S. Government Printing Office, 1967.

Reiser, M.: Some organizational stresses on policemen. *Journal of Police Science and Administration, 2* (2) :156-159, 1974.

Reiser, M.: *The Police Department Psychologist.* Springfield, Thomas, 1972.

Reiser, M.: *Practical Psychology for Police Officers.* Springfield, Thomas, 1973.

Reiss, A.: *The Police and the Public.* New Haven, Yale U Pr, 1971.

Rubin, J.: Police identity and the police role. In R. Steadman (Ed.) : *The Police and the Community.* Baltimore, Johns Hopkins University Press, 1972.

Rubin, J., and Cruse, D.: Police behavior (part II) . *Journal of Psychiatry and Law, 1* (3) :353-375, 1973.

Schwartz, J.: Single session crisis intervention: a new theoretical model. Paper presented at American Psychological Association Convention, Honolulu, September, 1972

Selye, H.: *Stress without Distress.* New York, Lippincott, 1974.

Selzer, M., and Vinokur, A.: Life events, subjective stress and accidents. Paper presented at the 126th Annual Meeting of the American Psychiatric Association, Honolulu, 1973.

Sherman, L. Milton, C., and Kelly, T.: *Team Policing.* Washington, D.C., Police Foundation, 1973.

Skolnick, J.: *Justice without Trial: Law Enforcement in Democratic Society.* New York, Wiley, 1967.

Special Task Force to the Secretary of Health, Education, and Welfare: *Work in America.* Cambridge, MIT Pr, 1973.

Sterling, J.: *Changes in Role Concepts of Police Officers.* Gaithersburg, International Association of Chiefs of Police, 1972.

Symonds, M.: Emotional hazards of police work. *Am J Psychoanal, 30* (2) : 155-160, 1970.

Symonds, M.: Policemen and policework: a psychodynamic understanding. *Am J. Psychoanal, 30* (2) :163-169, 1972.

Watson, N., and Sterling, J.: *Police and Their Opinions.* Gaithersburg, International Association of Chiefs of Police, 1969.

Whisenand, P., and Ferguson, F.: *The Managing of Police Organizations.* Englewood Cliffs, P-H, 1973.

Wilkinson, R.: Hours of work and the twenty-four hour cycle of rest and activity. In P. Warr (Ed.) : *Psychology at Work.* Middlesex, Penguin, 1971.

Wilson, J.: *Varieties of Police Behavior: The Management of Law and Order in Eight Communities.* New York, Atheneum, 1970.

Wilson, J.: The police in the ghetto. In R. Steadman (Ed.) : *The Police and the Community.* Baltimore, John Hopkins University Press, 1972.

Wilson, O.: *Police Administration.* New York, McGraw, 1963.

Zacker, J., and Bard, M.: Effects of conflict management training on police performance. *J Appl Psychol, 58* (2) :202-208, 1973.

Ziporyn, M.: Concert to courtroom to prison. Paper presented at Third Annual Stress Colloquium, American Academy of Stress Disorders, St. Charles, April, 1974.

INDEX